The Holy Spirit in the Bible

The Holy Spirit in the Bible

George M. Smiga

with Little Rock Scripture Study staff

LITURGICAL PRESS
Collegeville, Minnesota

www.littlerockscripture.org

Nihil obstat: Rev. Robert Harren, J.C.L., *Censor Librorum*.
Imprimatur: ✠ Most Rev. Donald J. Kettler, J.C.L., D.D., Bishop of St. Cloud, July 7, 2022.

Cover design by John Vineyard. Interior art by Ned Bustard. Photo and illustrations on page 16 courtesy of Liturgical Press Archives; pages 19, 37, 41, 67, 85, 95, and 98 courtesy of Getty Images.

This symbol indicates material that was created by Little Rock Scripture Study to supplement the biblical text and commentary. Some of these inserts first appeared in the *Little Rock Catholic Study Bible*; others were created specifically for this book by Amy Ekeh and George M. Smiga.

1	2	3	4	5	6	7	8	9

Library of Congress Cataloging-in-Publication Data

Names: Smiga, George M., 1948– author. | Little Rock Scripture Study Staff, author.
Title: The Holy Spirit in the Bible / George M. Smiga with Little Rock Scripture Study staff.
Description: Collegeville, MN : Liturgical Press, [2022] | Series: Little Rock scripture study | Summary: "This commentary explores the role of the Holy Spirit in people's lives and faith journeys through key Scripture passages. Commentary, study and reflection questions, prayers, and access to online lectures are included. 6 lessons"— Provided by publisher.
Identifiers: LCCN 2022017759 (print) | LCCN 2022017760 (ebook) | ISBN 9780814666630 (paperback) | ISBN 9780814666647 (epub) | ISBN 9780814666647 (pdf)
Subjects: LCSH: Holy Spirit—Biblical teaching—Textbooks. | Catholic Church—Doctrines—Textbooks.
Classification: LCC BT121.3 .S584 2022 (print) | LCC BT121.3 (ebook) | DDC 231/.3—dc23/eng/20220630
LC record available at https://lccn.loc.gov/2022017759
LC ebook record available at https://lccn.loc.gov/2022017760

TABLE OF CONTENTS

Wrap-Up Lectures and Discussion Tips for Facilitators are available for each lesson at no charge. Find them online at LittleRockScripture.org/Lectures/HolySpirit.

Welcome

The Bible is at the heart of what it means to be a Christian. It is the Spirit-inspired word of God for us. It reveals to us the God who created, redeemed, and guides us still. It speaks to us personally and as a church. It forms the basis of our public liturgical life and our private prayer lives. It urges us to live worthily and justly, to love tenderly and wholeheartedly, and to be a part of building God's kingdom here on earth.

Though it was written a long time ago, in the context of a very different culture, the Bible is no relic of the past. Catholic biblical scholarship is among the best in the world, and in our time and place, we have unprecedented access to it. By making use of solid scholarship, we can discover much about the ancient culture and religious practices that shaped those who wrote the various books of the Bible. With these insights, and by praying with the words of Scripture, we allow the words and images to shape us as disciples. By sharing our journey of faithful listening to God's word with others, we have the opportunity to be stretched in our understanding and to form communities of love and learning. Ultimately, studying and praying with God's word deepens our relationship with Christ.

The Holy Spirit in the Bible

The resource you hold in your hands is divided into six lessons. Each lesson involves personal prayer and study using this book and the experience of group prayer, discussion, and wrap-up lecture.

If you are using this resource in the context of a small group, we suggest that you meet six times, discussing one lesson per meeting. Allow about 90 minutes for the small group gathering. Small groups function best with eight to twelve people to ensure good group dynamics and to allow all to participate as they wish.

Some groups choose to have an initial gathering before their regular sessions begin. This allows an opportunity to meet one another, pass out books, and, if desired, view the optional intro lecture for this study available on the "Resources" page of the Little Rock Scripture Study website (www.littlerockscripture.org).

Every Bible study group is a little bit different. Some of our groups like to break each lesson up into two weeks of study so they are reading less each week and have more time to discuss the questions together at their weekly gatherings. If your group wishes to do this, simply agree how much of each lesson will be read each week, and only answer the questions that correspond to the material you read. Wrap-up lectures can then be viewed at the end of every other meeting rather than at the end of every meeting. Of course, this will mean that your study will last longer, and your group will meet more times.

WHAT MATERIALS WILL YOU USE?

The materials in this book include:

- Scripture passages to be studied, using the New American Bible, Revised Edition as the translation.
- Commentary by George M. Smiga.
- Occasional inserts ◉ highlighting elements of the Scripture passages being studied. Some of these appear also in the *Little Rock Catholic Study Bible* while others are supplied by the author and staff writers.
- Questions for study, reflection, and discussion at the end of each lesson.
- Opening and closing prayers for each lesson, as well as other prayer forms available in the closing pages of the book.

In addition, there are wrap-up lectures available for each lesson. Your group may choose to purchase a DVD containing these lectures or make use of the video lectures available online at no charge. The link to these free lectures is: LittleRockScripture.org/Lectures/HolySpirit. Of course, if your group has access to qualified speakers, you may choose to have live presentations.

Each person will need a current translation of the Bible. We recommend the *Little Rock Catholic Study Bible*, which makes use of the New American Bible, Revised Edition. Other translations, such as the New Jerusalem Bible or the New Revised Standard Version: Catholic Edition, would also work well.

HOW WILL YOU USE THESE MATERIALS?

Prepare in advance

Using Lesson One as an example:

- Begin with a simple prayer like the one found on page 11.

- Read the assigned material for Lesson One (pages 12–24) so that you are prepared for the weekly small group session.
- Answer the questions, Exploring Lesson One, found at the end of the assigned reading, pages 25–28.
- Use the Closing Prayer on page 28 when you complete your study. This prayer may be used again when you meet with the group.

Meet with your small group

- After introductions and greetings, allow time for prayer (about 5 minutes) as you begin the group session. You may use the prayer on page 11 (also used by individuals in their preparation) or use a prayer of your choosing.
- Spend about 45–50 minutes discussing the responses to the questions that were prepared in advance. You may also develop your discussion further by responding to questions and interests that arise during the discussion and faith-sharing itself.
- Close the discussion and faith-sharing with prayer, about 5–10 minutes. You may use the Closing Prayer at the end of each lesson or one of your choosing at the end of the book. It is important to allow people to pray for personal and community needs and to give thanks for how God is moving in your lives.
- Listen to or view the wrap-up lecture associated with each lesson (about 15 minutes). You may watch the lecture online, use a DVD, or provide a live lecture by a qualified local speaker. View the lecture together at the end of the session or, if your group runs out of time, you may invite group members to watch the lecture on their own time after the discussion.

A note to individuals

- If you are using this resource for individual study, simply move at your own pace. Take as much time as you need to read, study, and pray with the material.
- If you would like to share this experience with others, consider inviting a friend or family member to join you for your next study. Even a small group of two or three provides an opportunity for fruitful dialog and faith-sharing!

The Holy Spirit
in the Bible

LESSON ONE

The Holy Spirit at the Beginning

Begin your personal study and group discussion with a simple and sincere prayer such as:

Prayer

Spirit of God, you breathe life into human beings and into your Word. Fill us with your presence as we spend time with your Word and one another. Re-create us and sustain us day by day.

Read pages 12–24, Lesson One.

Respond to the questions on pages 25–28, Exploring Lesson One.

The Closing Prayer on page 28 is for your personal use and may be used at the end of group discussion.

INTRODUCTION

Christians are united in the belief that the Holy Spirit is God, the Third Person of the Most Holy Trinity. A full understanding of the Spirit, however, was not present at the beginning of our faith tradition. References to the Spirit of God are found throughout the Hebrew and Christian Scriptures. Yet only in the later writings of the New Testament do hints emerge that the Spirit is not an attribute of God but Someone.

The early centuries of church life were characterized by extensive debates over the natures of Jesus and the Spirit. The Council of Nicaea in 325 CE officially declared that Jesus is "one in being" (*homoousios*) with God the Father and is therefore fully God. The council's proclamation proved definitive and was in time universally accepted by Christians. Not until 381 CE did the Council of Constantinople assert that the same divine nature belonged to the Spirit, declaring the Holy Spirit to be "Lord and Giver of Life."

Therefore, as we begin this study of the Holy Spirit, we should not expect to discover scriptural passages that explicitly present the Spirit as the Third Person of the Trinity. What the Bible *does* offer is a variety of texts in which God's Spirit is shown to act. With the hindsight of the church's tradition, we are able to recognize these actions as the work of a Divine Person of the Godhead. To the biblical authors, however, the nature of the Spirit was less clear. For them, it was sufficient to focus on the Spirit as an aspect of God carrying out God's will in the world.

This study will examine biblical passages that describe the action of God's Spirit in the world and how such passages can speak to us today. Each of the six lessons will discuss a particular dimension of the Spirit's activity. Our approach will be chronological. Lesson One will present the Spirit acting in the process of creation, both cosmically and in the fashioning of the human person. We will then examine the Spirit's presence in those chosen by God to serve Israel (Lesson Two) and in Israel as a people (Lesson Three). The last three lessons will explore New Testament references to the Spirit. Lessons Four and Five will consider the Spirit in the ministry of Jesus and the early church. Lesson Six will conclude our study with the role of the Spirit at the end of time.

Within the limitations of this study, we are unable to examine every reference to the Spirit in the Bible. We will, however, address the major narratives and themes in which the Spirit appears. As we do this, it will soon become apparent that identifying the biblical passages that refer to the Spirit is complicated by vocabulary. For example, the word "spirit" in the Bible may sometimes refer to God's Spirit and other times may not. Choices must be made in interpreting the original text and the translations of it. We will discuss some of these instances as we go along.

In the following pages, you will encounter sections labeled "Contemporary Relevance." In them you will find suggestions for how a particular biblical passage may connect to our lives today. Examining the history, vocabulary, and theology of the Bible is important, but I believe it is of equal value to recognize how God's Spirit continues to guide us today. My suggestions in these sections should not be considered complete or definitive. I offer them only to encourage your own reflection on the role of the Spirit in your journey of faith.

THE HOLY SPIRIT AT THE BEGINNING

From Air to Divine Power

Names are important. They color the way the world is perceived. "Husband" and "Sweetheart" may refer to the same person, but each word carries its own nuance. Words are particularly crucial when they refer to God. As pure spirit, God cannot be seen or examined. In naming God, words must be drawn from human experience to capture even a hint of God's being. Words are always limited, yet they are the only means available to express what is inexpressible. The scriptural word for God's Spirit is a prime example of such a dynamic.

The Hebrew word for "spirit" describes a phenomenon of nature: a movement of air. The Hebrew term is *ruach*. It can be translated "wind" or "breath." Originally the term was used to describe a gentle breeze, a powerful storm, or the inhaling and exhaling of a living being. The Bible uses *ruach* to name such natural phenomena. But the way in which moving air can be sensed and yet remain unseen renders it a fitting metaphor for the action of the invisible God. The Scriptures often employ the word "spirit" in this "divine" sense. Sometimes, the use of *ruach* to describe God's actions must be discerned based on the context of the word in the biblical text, but frequently the divine sense is made explicit by linking *ruach* to the modifier "of God." Therefore, biblical translations will speak of "the wind of God," "the breath of God," and "the spirit of God." The Hebrew word *ruach* is behind all of these expressions.

To differentiate between *ruach* as a natural phenomenon (wind or breath) and *ruach* as God's Spirit, it would be helpful if the Bible always used the common designation of "Holy Spirit." But the Hebrew Bible (Old Testament) employs the modifier "holy" in only two places: Isaiah 63:10-11 and Psalm 51:13. In the New Testament, "Holy Spirit" is used more frequently, especially in the Gospels of Luke and John. Yet the expression "Holy Spirit" does not become commonplace until after the Council of Constantinople in 381 CE, centuries after the New Testament books were written. Therefore, as we read the biblical texts together, we will want to keep in mind that behind the words "wind," "breath," and "spirit" often stands the Holy Spirit of God.

 A note on the capitalization of "Spirit"

In any text describing God's Spirit, it must be decided whether the word "spirit" should be capitalized. When speaking of the Spirit in its fullest sense (as the Third Person of the Trinity) capitalization is certainly appropriate. In many scriptural passages, however, the view of the Spirit is less developed. For this reason, the New American Bible Revised Edition (NABRE), which is used throughout this study, does not capitalize "spirit" when it occurs in the Hebrew Bible (Old Testament). (See page 62 for information about capitalization in the New Testament.)

For clarity and consistency, however, we will capitalize "Spirit" throughout the commentary of this study when the word is used as a designation for God or an aspect of God. When the word "spirit" is used in a generic sense to designate *wind*, *breath*, or *spirit* and is not directly associated with the divine, "spirit" will be lowercase.

The Spirit Creates

The Bible assigns a role to God's Spirit in the formation of the world. Psalm 33:6 is a clear example: "By the LORD's word the heavens were made; / by the breath of his mouth all their host." Here, creation occurs through God's word and "the breath of his mouth." God's breath is the Spirit. The Bible also includes traces of a creation story in which God establishes the world by battling with a primeval sea serpent named Rahab. One of these passages is in the book of Job: "By his power he stilled Sea, / by his skill he crushed Rahab; / By his wind the heavens were made clear, / his hand pierced the fleeing serpent" (26:12-13). "[H]is wind" is another reference to God's Spirit at creation.

The Spirit plays a key role in the creation story at the beginning of the Bible. Genesis 1:1–2:3 describes the creation of the world in seven days. Here are the first three days of the narrative:

Genesis 1:1-13

The Story of Creation. ¹In the beginning, when God created the heavens and the earth— ²and the earth was without form or shape, with darkness over the abyss and a mighty wind sweeping over the waters—

³Then God said: Let there be light, and there was light. ⁴God saw that the light was good. God then separated the light from the darkness. ⁵God called the light "day," and the darkness he called "night." Evening came, and morning followed—the first day.

⁶Then God said: Let there be a dome in the middle of the waters, to separate one body of water from the other. ⁷God made the dome, and it separated the water below the dome from the water above the dome. And so it happened. ⁸God called the dome "sky." Evening came, and morning followed—the second day.

⁹Then God said: Let the water under the sky be gathered into a single basin, so that the dry land may appear. And so it happened: the water under the sky was gathered into its basin, and the dry land appeared. ¹⁰God called the dry land "earth," and the basin of water he called "sea." God saw that it was good. ¹¹Then God said: Let the earth bring forth vegetation: every kind of plant that bears seed and every kind of fruit tree on earth that bears fruit with its seed in it. And so it happened: ¹²the earth brought forth vegetation: every kind of plant that bears seed and every kind of fruit tree that bears fruit with its seed in it. God saw that it was good. ¹³Evening came, and morning followed—the third day.

The attentive reader will recognize the presence of the Spirit in verse 2: "a mighty wind sweeping over the waters." The Hebrew word for "wind," of course, is *ruach*. It is modified here by another word that can function as either an adjective or a possessive. If it is an adjective, the wind is being described as "awesome" or "mighty" (as in the translation above). If it functions as a possessive, the word can instead be rendered "divine" or "of God." As you might imagine, these options lead to a variety of translations. For example, the New American Bible Revised Edition (NABRE), which is the translation used in this study, gives us "a mighty wind." The New Revised Standard Version (NRSV) reads "a wind from God." The Jerusalem Bible prefers "a divine wind." The Jewish scholar, Robert Alter, translates the expression as "God's breath." And the New International Version (NIV) opts for "the Spirit of God." All of these translations are possible, and all designate God's action.

What exactly is this divine wind/breath/spirit doing? The NABRE says it is "sweeping over the waters." But, as usual, the Hebrew wording can lean in different directions. The Hebrew carries the sense of motion or vibration. Therefore, some translations indicate that the Spirit is "moving," "trembling," or "fluttering" above the waters. Other translators prefer to render the action of the Spirit as "hovering." This is because the same Hebrew word is used in the book of Deuteronomy to describe how God protects Israel: "As an eagle incites its nestlings, / *hovering* over its young, / So he spread his wings, took them, / bore them upon his pinions" (32:11; emphasis added). The translation "hovering," then, carries the sense of birthing and love. It is fitting to imagine the Spirit hovering over the primeval waters, ready to give life to the new creation.

 The **Babylonian creation myth** *Enuma Elish* is centuries older than Genesis 1. It presents the god Marduk in battle with a water-god, Tiamat. When Marduk slays Tiamat, he uses the pieces of her watery body to create the world. It is possible that this widely known story in the Ancient Near East influenced the authors of Genesis 1 to set God's action against the backdrop of a dark, watery deep that existed before God began to create (1:2). Many Ancient Near Eastern accounts characterize creation as an act of instilling order into chaos, a theme that also permeates Genesis 1.

Genesis 1 places God's Spirit at the very beginning of creation. Below we will consider three aspects of this narrative that speak about God's action and the Spirit at the beginning of time.

1) *Creation from nothing.* Christians believe that God created everything out of nothing. This truth is attested in 2 Maccabees 7:28 ("[L]ook at the heavens and the earth and see all that is in them; then you will know that God did not make them out of existing things") and Hebrews 11:3 ("By faith we understand that the universe was ordered by the word of God, so that what is visible came into being through the invisible").

Yet even accepting this truth, it is still possible to ask whether the creation story of Genesis 1 presents God creating from nothing. The answer is complicated. The first verse of Genesis can be translated in two different ways. If the words are read as a complete sentence, the Bible begins with a bold statement of God creating everything where nothing existed before. The NIV employs this option: "In the beginning

God created the heavens and the earth. Now the earth was formless and empty, darkness was over the surface of the deep, and the Spirit of God was hovering over the waters" (vv. 1-2). But Genesis 1:1 can also be translated as an opening phrase with the sense of "when." In this reading, God creates not out of nothing but out of the formless stuff that is already there. The NABRE chooses this option (see p. 14).

Utilizing preexisting primeval matter was a common trait of the creation stories of the Ancient Near East. The authors of Genesis 1 were likely familiar with this characterization and would not have been opposed to descriptions of the God of Israel acting this way. The opening verses of the Bible are therefore ambiguous. They can be understood as God creating out of nothing or out of what already existed.

Contemporary Relevance: This ambiguity in the narrative of Genesis 1:1-2 offers rich interpretive possibilities. It suggests that when God acts to bring new life to our world, God is not limited to one manner of creation. Sometimes God crafts new life out of things that already exist, and other times God brings life out of nothing. When a close relationship with a spouse or friend is hanging by a thread, God can inject new life by building on something in the relationship that is already there: a common interest, a shared dream, or dormant feelings of love that can be rekindled. But God can also introduce something totally new. A deep experience of joy can fundamentally change both people and provide a fresh starting point. The pain of a shared loss can allow all involved to see life from a new perspective. We need not decide whether or not God creates out of nothing. God's Spirit, hovering over us, is ready to build upon what exists or to surprise us with a new creation.

2) *Protection from chaos.* To fully appreciate the narrative of Genesis 1, we must understand the cosmological view of its biblical authors. Their ancient view of the universe helps us understand their description of God's act of creating. God is described as separating one thing from another—light from darkness (v. 4), water from water (v. 6), day from night (v. 14). This separating is necessary because the authors of

Genesis 1 envisioned their contemporary world surrounded by chaotic waters. They believed there was water above the sky. This is how they accounted for rain. When they came to a large body of water and could not see the other side, it was easy for them to imagine that the water went on forever. They believed that dry land sat in the midst of such waters, floating above a watery deep. God's action of creation in Genesis 1 has been drawn in light of this world-view. God is presented as pushing back the waters of chaos to establish a dry place where animals and humans can live.

This cosmological view is shown most clearly on the second and third days of creation. Having separated light from darkness, God creates "a dome in the middle of the waters, to separate one body of water from the other" (v. 6). This "dome" is the sky (v. 8). It separates the waters above the sky from the waters below it. Then God separates the waters below the sky from each other so that dry land can appear (v. 9). The waters that God separates are destructive, hostile to human life. They are "the abyss" or "the deep" that were covered in darkness when God began to create. These are the waters of chaos over which the breath of God moved at the beginning of time (v. 2). Genesis 1 portrays God's act of creation as setting boundaries to this primal disarray, keeping the chaos at bay. In the beginning there is disorder, a watery mess. Then God speaks, and there is light, a dome to separate the waters, and dry land. The original chaos is still there, but now it is subservient to God's control.

Contemporary Relevance: We no longer view our earth as the ancient Hebrews did. Rain results from condensation. One sea leads to another. Our continents do not float over a watery deep. But we do know what chaos is, whether it be mental, spiritual, political, or environmental. When chaos erupts, the livable order of our lives is overturned. Chaos can burst forth after diagnosis of a serious illness or the death of a loved one. It can gush out when a friend or family member hurts us or when we experience financial distress. Instead of living a secure life,

we find ourselves struggling to stay afloat in troubled waters that try to pull us down.

In such moments, the creation account of Genesis 1 reminds us that our God is the master over chaos. God's power is more than equal to the forces that can turn our lives into turmoil and madness. God does not promise to eliminate all chaos from our lives but only to restrain it from destroying us. We still may have to maintain contact with the friend or family member who hurt us or cope with the effects of a worldwide pandemic. But God has set limits that chaos cannot cross. God promises there will be dry land on which to live, air for us to breathe. Like the ancient Hebrews, we exist in a world where watery disorder surrounds us. But God's ever-present, ever-creating Spirit provides enough safe space so we can grow, love, and build a future.

3) *The world is good.* Seven times in Genesis 1, God sees creation as "good" (vv. 4, 10, 12, 18, 21, 25, and 31). The description serves as a refrain of the creation story. After calling a particular part of the world into being, God assesses its success. The judgment is always positive. The Hebrew word for "good" used in this chapter

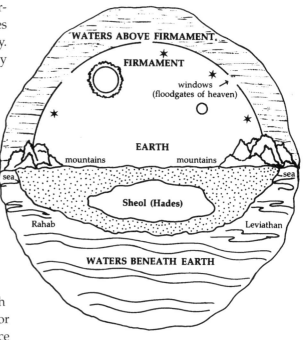

The world of the ancient Hebrews

16

is *towb*. Like the English word "good," it carries a wide range of meaning. People and things can be good in a variety of ways. Good can be aesthetic, spiritual, behavioral, moral, emotional, and interpersonal—to mention only some aspects. Resonances of all these positive dimensions can be heard when God assesses creation as "good." God is saying that what has just been made is exactly as it should be. The expression is not without a sense of delight, a certain playfulness. God steps back from creating, looks at what has been made, and in essence says, "Perfect! This makes me happy."

Contemporary Relevance: God's evaluation of creation in Genesis 1 is an invitation for us to rejoice in our world. It is a call to wonder at the goodness that God has made, to see the perfection of a finger, a snowflake, or a star. We can and should marvel at our ability to understand, communicate, and love. In a time when we are increasingly aware of the threats to our environment, this Genesis narrative reminds us that beneath the pollution and abuse lies a world of freshness and beauty. We are closest to God's intention when we delight in the planet that is our home, taking in the warmth of the sun, the power of a storm, or the smell of the earth after an April rain. If God paused each day of creation to rejoice at what had been made through the Spirit, we must not be too busy or preoccupied to do the same.

The Spirit and the Great Flood

It might seem peculiar to move from the beautiful creation account of Genesis 1 to the devastating flood of Genesis 6–8. But the two stories are closely related. In the first, God creates. In the second, creation is undone. The flood described in these chapters is not a huge rainstorm. It is a return to the watery mess that was present before God made the world. The text is clear. When the flood begins, we are told, "All the fountains of the great abyss burst forth, / and the floodgates of the sky were opened" (7:11). The "abyss" is the primeval sea under the earth, and the "floodgates" hold back the waters above the dome. The careful separation of waters that God established on the second and third days of creation (1:6-10) is being erased. The world is returning to chaos.

 The story of the flood in Genesis bears a strong resemblance to *Atrahasis*, an earlier **flood story of ancient Mesopotamia**. In that story, the gods regret making humans and decide to wipe them out using a universal flood. One man, Atrahasis, builds a boat and rides out the flood. After the flood ends, the gods create humanity anew. The parallels to Genesis are obvious. But so are the differences. In *Atrahasis*, the gods send the flood because humans were too noisy and kept the gods awake. They re-create because they miss the humans who served their needs. In Genesis, God sends the flood because of human wickedness and then promises never to do so again because of the love God bears for humanity.

In the Hebrew Scriptures, the destruction of creation is occasioned by God's grief. God desires a relationship with the world, but creation refuses to comply:

Genesis 6:5-7

Warning of the Flood. [5]When the LORD saw how great the wickedness of human beings was on earth, and how every desire that their heart conceived was always nothing but evil, [6]the LORD regretted making human beings on the earth, and his heart was grieved.

[7]So the LORD said: I will wipe out from the earth the human beings I have created, and not only the human beings, but also the animals and the crawling things and the birds of the air, for I regret that I made them.

God planned to delight in the created world, but because of human wickedness, God decides to scrap the plan of Genesis 1, going so far as to "wipe out" *all* living things (v. 7).

In this story, God is changeable. Traditional Christian theology does not accept change in God. God is understood to be all knowing and all powerful. What God decides is perfect and lasting. But this biblical story humanizes (anthropomorphizes) God. In an effort to portray God's deep desire to relate to creation, the narrative describes God as grieving and even regretting. Divine love has been rejected by human beings. God concludes that the original plan for creation has failed.

But the good news in this story is that God changes more than once. In Genesis 8:1-3, God alters the plan again:

Genesis 8:1-3

God remembered Noah and all the animals, wild and tame, that were with him in the ark. So God made a wind sweep over the earth, and the waters began to subside. [2]The fountains of the abyss and the floodgates of the sky were closed, and the downpour from the sky was held back. [3]Gradually the waters receded from the earth.

Remembering the goodness of Noah and all living things, God gives creation a second chance. God will again push back the waters of chaos. In 8:1, a wind sweeps over the earth. The wind is *ruach*, God's Spirit. Just as the Spirit hovered over the chaos at the first creation (1:2), here the wind of God again allows dry land to appear.

The reason for God's decision to push back the waters is given after Noah leaves the ark and offers sacrifice: "When the LORD smelled the sweet odor, the LORD said to himself: Never again will I curse the ground because of human beings, since the desires of the human heart are evil from youth; nor will I ever again strike down every living being, as I have done" (8:21). This verse reveals to us the inner decision of God. Never again will God destroy the earth.

God's reasoning is stunning. Aware that humans are inclined to evil, God decides not to allow that inclination to win. Humanity will not change, so God will. Even if humanity continues to sin, God will continue to love. Even if creation does not respond, God will maintain the relationship and rejoice in what was made. Genesis 8:21 reveals a God of unilateral and unconditional love, anticipating God's saving action in Jesus. As Paul says in Romans 5:8, "But God proves his love for us in that while we were still sinners Christ died for us."

Contemporary Relevance: As disciples of Christ, we know well what God expects of us. We are to love God and neighbor, promote justice, forgive our enemies, and preserve life, especially the lives of the most vulnerable members of our society. God's expectations are real. But God is prepared for our failure. The decision of God after the flood asserts God's willingness to be in relationship with us on unequal terms. We will always be the weaker partner. We will always be unable to match God's faithfulness and love. But Genesis 8:21 assures us that God is fully prepared for such a lopsided relationship. God is willing to receive our compromised efforts to love, our half-hearted attempts to forgive, and our tepid efforts to build a better world. This is the good news in the story of the flood. From the time God's Spirit pushes back the chaotic waters a second time, God understands how the relationship with humanity will play out. We will try to live up to the goodness given to us at creation, and we will repeatedly fail. But God will not be deterred. God will love and redeem us still.

The Spirit in History

The Bible is clear that the role of the Spirit of God does not end with creation. The work of the Spirit continues in history—saving, sustaining, forgiving, and guiding what God has made.

The great saving event for Israel was the exodus from Egypt. So important was this deliverance that Israel told the story over and over, in a variety of ways. Chapter 14 of Exodus describes the most famous version, in which the waters of the sea are split and the Israelites cross between two great walls of water. Chapter 15 includes a poetic and likely more ancient version in which the churning of the waters as they rushed in upon the pursuing Egyptians is described as a great storm. This is how the event is described:

Exodus 15:3-10

[3]The LORD is a warrior,
  LORD is his name!
[4]Pharaoh's chariots and army he hurled into
    the sea;
  the elite of his officers were drowned in
    the Red Sea.
[5]The flood waters covered them,
  they sank into the depths like a stone.
[6]Your right hand, O LORD, magnificent in
    power,
  your right hand, O LORD, shattered the
    enemy.

[7]In your great majesty you overthrew your
    adversaries;
  you loosed your wrath to consume them
    like stubble.
[8]At the blast of your nostrils the waters
    piled up,
  the flowing waters stood like a mound,
  the flood waters foamed in the midst of
    the sea.
[9]The enemy boasted, "I will pursue and
    overtake them;
  I will divide the spoils and have my fill of
    them;
  I will draw my sword; my hand will
    despoil them!"
[10]When you blew with your breath, the sea
    covered them;
  like lead they sank in the mighty waters.

The Spirit is present as God saves the chosen people from bondage. The "blast" of verse 8 and the "breath" of verse 10 are translations of *ruach,* the powerful, saving Spirit of God.

The stormy defeat of Pharaoh's armies at the Red Sea (Exodus 15)

The action of the Spirit is attested again when the Israelites, now liberated from slavery, journey to the Promised Land. When the people complain that they are starving in the desert, God feeds them. Numbers 11:31-32 relates the scene:

Numbers 11:31-32

The Quail. [31]There arose a wind from the LORD that drove in quail from the sea and left them all around the camp site, to a distance of a day's journey and at a depth of two cubits upon the ground. [32]So all that day, all night, and all the next day the people set about to gather in the quail. Even the one who got the least gathered ten homers of them. Then they spread them out all around the camp.

A homer is a dry measure roughly equal to what a donkey can carry. This generous gift comes through "a wind from the LORD," which is God's sustaining Spirit.

God's Spirit does not only save and sustain the community. Individuals also benefit from the Spirit's assistance. A psalm found in 2 Samuel (and paralleled in Psalm 18) describes God's saving power toward a person in need of protection. God's deliverance is described in dramatic terms:

---

2 Samuel 22:14-18

[14]The LORD thundered from heaven;
    the Most High made his voice resound.
[15]He let fly arrows and scattered them;
    lightning, and dispersed them.
[16]Then the bed of the sea appeared;
    the world's foundations lay bare,
At the roar of the LORD,
    at the storming breath of his nostrils.
[17]He reached down from on high and seized me,
    drew me out of the deep waters.

---

[18]He rescued me from my mighty enemy,
    from foes too powerful for me.

The rescue of the psalmist is described in words echoing the creation account in Genesis. The world's foundations are laid bare by the "breath" of the Lord's nostrils, God's Spirit (v.16).

God's Spirit is also active when sin must be forgiven. This saving activity of the Spirit is described in the prayer of Psalm 51:11-14: "Turn away your face from my sins; / blot out all my iniquities. / A clean heart create for me, God; / renew within me a steadfast spirit. / Do not drive me from before your face, / nor take from me your holy spirit. / Restore to me the gladness of your salvation; / uphold me with a willing spirit." Notice the beautiful interplay between the psalmist's spirit and God's Spirit. The psalmist prays that his spirit becomes "steadfast" and "willing," but it is clear that such a condition depends upon the gift of God's own Spirit.

Psalm 143:10 presents the Spirit as a guide: "Teach me to do your will, / for you are my God. / May your kind spirit guide me / on ground that is level." Moreover, access to this guiding Spirit is not limited to any time or place. Psalm 139:7-8 uses a series of questions to establish this truth: "Where can I go from your spirit? / From your presence, where can I flee? / If I ascend to the heavens, you are there; / if I lie down in Sheol, there you are." The universal presence of the Spirit is extolled at length in Psalm 104. The hymn enumerates the heavens, earth, clouds, mountains, springs, sun, moon, grass, trees, birds, wild goats, badgers, lions, and human beings in an attempt to express the diversity of creation. All that exists depends upon God's Spirit for food and life. In summary, Psalm 104:30 prays, "Send forth your spirit, they are created / and you renew the face of the earth." God's Spirit does much more than create. The Spirit saves, sustains, forgives, and guides all that God has made, making it ever new.

The Spirit as God's Breath within the Human Person

As has already been discussed, the Hebrew word for "spirit" originally named the phenomenon of moving air. Human breath is moving air at its most personal. If there is not the movement of breathing, human life does not exist. When the biblical writers wanted to express the transitory nature of life, they associated life with a breath: "Man is but a breath, / his days are like a passing shadow" (Ps 144:4; see also Ps 39:6, 12; 62:10). Genesis 6:3 offers an explanation for the limits of human life and asserts its source: "Then the Lord said: My spirit shall not remain in human beings forever, because they are only flesh. Their days shall comprise one hundred and twenty years."

The Jewish belief in creation recognized that the breath of life, which animates all creatures, comes from God. Job 12:10 says, "In his hand is the soul of every living thing, / and the life breath of all mortal flesh" (see also Zech 12:1). Ecclesiastes 12:7, in describing death, shares the same perspective: "And the dust returns to the earth as it once was, / and the life breath returns to God who gave it" (see also Isa 57:16 and Wis 15:11).

Since God is the origin of human life and breath, it is an easy step for the Scriptures to identify human breath with God's breath. Humans breathe to live. But the breath within them is the breath of God. Job 27:3-4 illustrates this: "So long as I still have life breath in me, / the breath of God in my nostrils, / My lips shall not speak falsehood, / nor my tongue utter deceit!" The point is made even stronger in Job 33:4: "For the spirit of God made me, / the breath of the Almighty keeps me alive." Fittingly, God's breath not only gives life but also allows humans to know and understand: "But there is a spirit in human beings, / the breath of the Almighty, that gives them understanding" (Job 32:8).

The belief that God's very breath is within the human person expresses a striking intimacy between God and humanity. Here, *ruach* becomes a relational term. It not only identifies "breath" as the principle of life, but it also implies that because human breath is God's breath, humans exist in a dynamic relationship with God.

The most visual description of this relationship occurs within the second creation account of the Bible. Genesis 2:4-25 is a creation story that is older and displays a different focus and theology than the creation account in Genesis 1:

Genesis 2:4-25

The Garden of Eden. [4]This is the story of the heavens and the earth at their creation. When the Lord God made the earth and the heavens— [5]there was no field shrub on earth and no grass of the field had sprouted, for the Lord God had sent no rain upon the earth and there was no man to till the ground, [6]but a stream was welling up out of the earth and watering all the surface of the ground— [7]then the Lord God formed the man out of the dust of the ground and blew into his nostrils the breath of life, and the man became a living being.

[8]The Lord God planted a garden in Eden, in the east, and placed there the man whom he had formed. [9]Out of the ground the Lord God made grow every tree that was delightful to look at and good for food, with the tree of life in the middle of the garden and the tree of the knowledge of good and evil.

[10]A river rises in Eden to water the garden; beyond there it divides and becomes four branches. [11]The name of the first is the Pishon; it is the one that winds through the whole land of Havilah, where there is gold. [12]The gold of that land is good; bdellium and lapis lazuli are also there. [13]The name of the second river is the Gihon; it is the one that winds all through the land of Cush. [14]The name of the third river is the Tigris; it is the one that flows east of Asshur. The fourth river is the Euphrates.

[15]The Lord God then took the man and settled him in the garden of Eden, to cultivate and care for it. [16]The Lord God gave the man this

continue

---

order: You are free to eat from any of the trees of the garden ¹⁷except the tree of knowledge of good and evil. From that tree you shall not eat; when you eat from it you shall die.

¹⁸The LORD God said: It is not good for the man to be alone. I will make a helper suited to him. ¹⁹So the LORD God formed out of the ground all the wild animals and all the birds of the air, and he brought them to the man to see what he would call them; whatever the man called each living creature was then its name. ²⁰The man gave names to all the tame animals, all the birds of the air, and all the wild animals; but none proved to be a helper suited to the man.

²¹So the LORD God cast a deep sleep on the man, and while he was asleep, he took out one of his ribs and closed up its place with flesh. ²²The LORD God then built the rib that he had taken from the man into a woman. When he brought her to the man, ²³the man said:

"This one, at last, is bone of my bones
and flesh of my flesh;
This one shall be called 'woman,'
for out of man this one has been taken."

²⁴That is why a man leaves his father and mother and clings to his wife, and the two of them become one body.

²⁵The man and his wife were both naked, yet they felt no shame.

Genesis 2:10-14 may be an originally independent account that was later inserted into Genesis 2 by biblical editors. These verses tell us that a single river waters Paradise and then divides into four rivers in the geographical world. The number four implies that the rivers are meant to enumerate all the rivers which cover the "four corners" of the earth. The meaning of the passage flows from this realization. Water is essential to life. Genesis 2:10-14 asserts that the life-giving power that comes from the world's rivers is a gift from the original Paradise.

Whereas the account of Genesis 1 presents the formation of the various structures of the world, the story of Genesis 2 focuses upon the human person. It does not describe how God formed the sky, bodies of water, or heavenly bodies. In fact, Genesis 2 is less concerned about how things came to be and more interested in exploring how humanity is to live as a part of creation. In this regard, the creation of the human person takes center stage. In Genesis 1, God creates man and woman by divine decree: "Let us make human beings in our image, after our likeness" (v. 26). In Genesis 2:7, God creates not by a declaration from on high but by fash-

ioning the first human from the dust of the ground. In this scene, God can be appropriately pictured as a potter, forming something new from common clay. But once God's work has been shaped, it still has to live. So God blows into the nostrils of what was made "the breath of life." Note that the word used in Genesis 2:7 for "breath" is not *ruach* but *neshamah*, an earlier poetic word that carries the same meaning. The human person comes to life by receiving God's breath, the Spirit of God.

Contemporary Relevance: The creation of the human person in Genesis 2 is a profoundly influential passage, both in the Bible and in our lives. We will see several biblical authors refer to it in later lessons of this book. As to its relevance for our own faith, here are three suggestions to begin your reflection.

1) *Human dignity.* The belief that we carry within us the breath of God instills a fundamental dignity to every human person. People may be characterized as wounded, physically or mentally challenged, strangers, or even enemies. But prior to any of these qualifications, every person breathes. The movement of inhaling and exhaling is the indication of God's indwelling, the movement of God's Spirit. Therefore, dismissal of or violence toward any human person is an assault against the very life of God. Whenever we encounter another

person, the Spirit of God is in the air. Human breath should remind us of where God is found.

2) *Naming as creation.* Once the breath of God is given to the clay creature that God has made, the new being shares in God's power. This is shown in the remarkable passage in which God first forms the animals and then brings them to the human to be named (v. 19). Naming is a sign of control and power. In Genesis 1, God names the day, night, sky, earth, and sea. In Genesis 2, the power of naming is given to the newly formed human. Assigning a name is much more than associating a word with a creature. It is the way we organize our world. Once a creature is named, it assumes a specific place in human life. This truth is captured in the text: "whatever the man called each living creature was then its name" (v. 19). When a wild animal becomes a "cow" or a bird of the air becomes a "nightingale," it is no longer simply another creature but a creature that carries a particular meaning for us. Naming reshapes our world. It is an additional act of creation.

Naming continues to create our world. Its power can be used for good or ill. When we name a person a "sister" or "friend," that person assumes an important place in our personal existence. When we tag someone an "enemy" or "fool," he or she is relegated to another sphere of our lives. Our world tends to shrink when it is populated with people who are "weak," "compromised," or "untrustworthy." Our joy expands when we live among those who are "creative," "talented," and "fun." People do not simply exist "as they are." They live through the names we choose to assign them. This is why it is important to choose names carefully. Names should be given in honesty and fairness. The stakes are high. The names we assign to others create the world in which we all must live.

3) *The need for intimacy.* Genesis 2 centers on humanity's place in creation, highlighting human gifts and needs. It is clear that what humans need above all is intimacy. Finding such unique companionship is the center of

this story. The problem emerges in verse 18, when God recognizes, "It is not good for the man to be alone." This begins the quest to find a "helper" for the newly formed human. The Hebrew word for "helper" is not to be understood in a demeaning way, such as being "an assistant." The word denotes help in the sense of "saving" and is often used in the Bible to describe God's action toward us. Here is how Isaiah 41:10 presents God's helping: "Do not fear: I am with you; / do not be anxious: I am your God. / I will strengthen you, I will help you, / I will uphold you with my victorious right hand." So the helper that God wants to provide is a companion who is able to share life with the human and offer saving support. The animals God created are not able to help in this way (v. 20).

This is why God creates a woman and brings her to the man, who cannot live alone (v. 22). Here the narrative reaches its climax. The man recognizes a unique intimacy with God's newest creation. Both are alive through God's Spirit. Both share the same bone and flesh (v. 23). Such closeness, on a literal level, results from the new creature having been formed from the man's own body. But the narrative is also meant to

Whenever we encounter another person, the Spirit of God is in the air.

address our present experience. It asserts that every person is made to find intimacy with others. Verse 24 clearly associates this intimacy with marriage (as does Jesus in Mark 10:6-9). Yet the need for intimacy should not be limited to marriage. If God's purpose in human creation is to be met, every person must discover some intimate relationship. This need not be a spousal relationship; a sibling or friend can become a partner close enough to be "bone of my bones / and flesh of my flesh" (Gen 2:23). This narrative emphasizes that without deep human relationships, creation is incomplete.

When presented with the woman, the man speaks for the first time: "This one, at last, is bone of my bones / and flesh of my flesh" (v. 23). This is the first time anyone other than God speaks in the Bible. The words are an exclamation of joy, extolling and proclaiming God's unique gift. The man then names the new creation "woman." This is not like the naming of the animals. This is the naming of the one with whom the man will share life. The Hebrew text is remarkably sophisticated here. The word for woman is *ishshah*. It echoes the Hebrew word for man, *ish*. (Much like in English, the word "woman" includes the word "man.") The similarity of the Hebrew words indicates that woman is man's equal because, unlike the animals, their names are intimately connected.

But the implications of this story do not end here. Up to this point in the Hebrew text, the first human has not been called "man" (*ish*). Because he was formed from the dust of the earth, he has been referred to by a Hebrew word best translated as "earth creature." It is only in verse 23, when the new creature is named "woman" (*ishshah*), that the "earth creature" is called "man" (*ish*).

This complexity of vocabulary carries a profound message. When God gifts us with an intimate relationship, we are changed. When we, like the first human, claim another person as God's gift, when we embrace another as a spouse or close friend, that claim and embrace unlock new dimensions of our personalities. God's Spirit moves within us. We understand love and life more deeply. We appreciate who we are through the eyes of another. We visualize our purpose and our dreams more clearly. When the creature that God formed from the dust names woman, he discovers his own existence as man. When we, in gratitude, accept another into a deep and meaningful relationship, we—perhaps for the first time—understand who we are.

EXPLORING LESSON ONE

1. a) The introduction to this study states that we will not find Scripture passages that present the Spirit of God as the Third Person of the Trinity. Why is this the case?

_____

_____

_____

_____

_____

   b) What *do* the Scriptures tell us about God's Spirit? In what ways do you imagine such insights will be helpful to you?

_____

_____

_____

_____

_____

2. Why does the Hebrew word for "spirit" (*ruach*) make it difficult to determine when the Bible is referring to the Holy Spirit? Why is *ruach* an appropriate image for the Holy Spirit?

_____

_____

_____

_____

_____

3. How would you describe what God's Spirit is doing at creation (Gen 1:1-2)? Did the commentary on these verses provide you with any new insight or raise any new questions for you?

_____

_____

_____

_____

_____

4. The authors of Genesis viewed the arrangement of the cosmos in a dramatically different way from our present scientific understanding. How does "the dome" in Genesis 1:6-8 serve God's purpose of creating a safe place for creation to exist? How might this protective act of God still speak to us today?

_____

_____

_____

_____

_____

_____

5. Throughout Genesis 1, creation is affirmed as good and beautiful to God. When, if ever, has the beauty, power, or wonder of the created world brought you closer to God's Spirit?

_____

_____

_____

_____

_____

_____

6. a) Why might the story of the flood in Genesis 6–8 be called an "un-creation story"? How is God's Spirit active in this narrative?

_____

_____

_____

_____

_____

b) How do the biblical authors use the story of the flood to reveal God's eternal commitment to remain in relationship with us? What does the story tell us about the terms of that relationship?

_____

_____

_____

_____

_____

7. After creation God's Spirit saves, sustains, forgives, and guides. How have you recognized the activity of the Spirit in any of these dimensions of your own life?

_____

_____

_____

_____

_____

_____

_____

8. How do we understand the description of the Spirit as "breath" in such passages as Job 32:8 and 33:4? How might this insight influence the way we view every human person, including those we dislike or find difficult to understand?

_____

_____

_____

_____

_____

_____

_____

9. a) In what way is the role of the Spirit in Genesis 2 more intimate than in Genesis 1?

_____

_____

_____

_____

b) What does Adam's ability to name animals say about his relationship to God and to the rest of creation? In what sense does the power of naming continue in our own lives?

_____

_____

_____

_____

_____

10. The commentary provides insight into how Genesis 2 speaks to our relationships today, regardless of our state in life. What further insights about human beings or the Spirit can you share based on your own reflections on this creation account?

_____

_____

_____

_____

_____

CLOSING PRAYER

Prayer

"For the spirit of God made me,
the breath of the Almighty keeps me alive."

(Job 33:4)

Spirit of God, you create, you re-create, and you give life. You breathe into each one of us the breath of your own being, and we live because you sustain us. May we never take this gift of life for granted, but may we recognize your sacred presence in ourselves and in every human being. We pray today for those who doubt their own worth, that they may be assured they are created, loved, and sustained by the life and breath of God's own Spirit. We also pray today for . . .

LESSON TWO

The Holy Spirit and Individual Israelites

Begin your personal study and group discussion with a simple and sincere prayer such as:

Prayer

Spirit of God, you breathe life into human beings and into your Word. Fill us with your presence as we spend time with your Word and one another. Re-create us and sustain us day by day.

Read pages 30–41, Lesson Two.

Respond to the questions on pages 42–44, Exploring Lesson Two.

The Closing Prayer on page 44 is for your personal use and may be used at the end of group discussion.

THE HOLY SPIRIT AND INDIVIDUAL ISRAELITES

In the Hebrew Bible, individuals chosen by God to act on behalf of the people are often said to be filled with the Spirit of God. This lesson will examine the Spirit's presence in some of these individuals of Israel: two artisans, two judges, two kings, and a patriarch. We will also consider the story of one non-Israelite, a seer named Balaam. Through these biblical accounts, we will see how the same Spirit who breathed life into the first human at creation continues to guide the work of human artistry, provide assurance to those who lack confidence, raise up unexpected leaders, deepen understanding, and bring reconciliation to fractured families. Indeed, the depth and diversity of the Spirit's action is as wide as creation itself.

The Spirit and Artisans: Bezalel and Oholiab

Exodus 25–31 provides instructions for the building of a portable ark in which God will dwell during the journey to the Promised Land. In Exodus 31:1-6, God chooses two men, Bezalel and Oholiab, to construct the ark:

Exodus 31:1-6

Choice of Artisans. [1]The LORD said to Moses: [2]See, I have singled out Bezalel, son of Uri, son of Hur, of the tribe of Judah, [3]and I have filled him with a divine spirit of skill and understanding and knowledge in every craft: [4]in the production of embroidery, in making things of gold, silver, or bronze, [5]in cutting and mounting precious stones, in carving wood, and in every other craft. [6]As his assistant I myself have appointed Oholiab, son of Ahisamach, of the tribe of Dan. I have also endowed all the experts with the necessary skill to make all the things I have commanded you:

Even though Oholiab is called an "assistant" in the above translation, the Hebrew is literally "I have given with him." This indicates that Oholiab and Bezalel are to work together, both fully knowledgeable of all crafts. Thus both men are filled with "a *divine spirit* of skill and understanding and knowledge in every craft" (v. 3; emphasis added). The Spirit of God is given to them to enable their work.

This passage exalts the work of Bezalel and Oholiab. The reference to the "divine spirit" in them recalls the presence of the Spirit at creation. "Spirit" here is again *ruach*. It occurs in verse 3 with the same modifier used in Genesis 1:2, making it a "divine spirit" and the same Spirit that swept over the waters at the beginning of the world (see p. 14).

Moreover, the two men are given "skill and understanding and knowledge." The Hebrew word for "skill" can also be translated as "wisdom." Proverbs 3:19-20 closely associates all three terms with creation: "The LORD by *wisdom* founded the earth, / established the heavens by *understanding*; / By his *knowledge* the depths are split, / and the clouds drop down dew" (emphasis added; see also Ps 104:24; Prov 8:22-31; Sir 1:6-10). The skilled work of Bezalel and Oholiab is a continuation of creation, a gift of God's *ruach*.

Contemporary Relevance: This text gives human artistry a deep, even divine, significance. When something beautiful is fashioned by human hands, it extends God's creation. When we are moved by the power of music, the impact of drama, or the exhilaration of dance, God's Spirit is at work. When we say that a painting, a poem, or a glass of wine is good, we echo God in Genesis 1, who saw all creation as good. What God began, artisans of every time and place continue.

The Spirit influences every genuine artistic accomplishment. Exodus 31:1-6 pertains to a religious undertaking, the building of God's dwelling. But the role of the Spirit is not limited to sacred art. The text suggests this wider understanding. Verse 6 reads, "I have also endowed all the experts with the necessary skill." A more literal translation of the Hebrew is "I have given skill to all the skillful." The Hebrew text purposefully uses the same word twice, communicating that skill is given to those who are already skillful. In other words, the infusion of God's Spirit animates a natural ability that is already present. A supernatural gift resides within a human capacity. Therefore, any art that is genuinely human is already blessed by God. The artistic work need not be religious, nor must the artist be a person of religious faith. The divine dimension of artistic creation is grounded in a previous gift: the breath of life, first given when God's Spirit swept over the waters.

The Spirit and the Judges of Israel: Gideon

Before Israel was governed by a monarchy, it was ruled by men and women called "judges." These individuals did not preside over courts of law. They were charismatic leaders raised up by God to save Israel. Their exploits are recorded in the book of Judges. The narrative of each judge follows a set pattern: the people sin, their enemies dominate over them, God provides a judge to defeat the enemies and restore tranquility, and peace continues until the judge dies. The cycle then repeats.

Four of Israel's judges are explicitly described as being empowered by the Spirit of God. God calls Othniel through the Spirit: "The spirit of the Lord came upon him, and he judged Israel" (Judg 3:10). The Spirit also descends upon the judge Jephthah in Judges 11:29. The other two Spirit-filled judges are Gideon and Samson. Their stories will be examined more fully.

 In Hebrew, the name **"Gideon" means "hacker."** It describes the action of Gideon in "hacking down" the altar of Baal in Judges 6:25-32. In English, "hacker" can be used in two different ways. It can refer to "someone unskilled at an activity," but it can also name "an expert at programming and solving problems with a computer." Such a difference in meaning perfectly suits the story of Gideon, who, although perfectly capable in God's sight, struggles to accept his own abilities.

In the Hebrew Bible, Gideon receives more attention than any other judge. His exploits fill chapters 6–8 in the book of Judges. God sees Gideon as eminently qualified to save Israel. But Gideon sees himself as weak and inadequate, and he questions his ability to serve as a judge. In Judges 6:7-24, God calls Gideon to defeat the Midianites, who were oppressing Israel. From God's perspective, Gideon is a "mighty warrior" (v. 12) with the strength to save Israel (v. 14). But Gideon objects, "My family is the poorest in Manasseh, and I am the most insignificant in my father's house" (v. 15). Commentators have pointed out that, contrary to Gideon's claims, Manasseh was a highly prestigious tribe, and Gideon was not without resources. In 6:27, for example, Gideon has the means to single out ten men from his large entourage of servants. However, the issue of the narrative is not whether Gideon is capable and worthy but whether he is able to accept himself as such. This explains why a sizable portion of Gideon's story is devoted to divine signs of assurance.

Three times Gideon asks God to verify that he is up to the call. When God first appears, Gideon asks for a sign to prove that his call is genuine (6:17). In response, an angel summons fire from a rock to consume the meat and unleavened cakes Gideon had set upon it (6:21). Gideon then agrees to lead the forces of Israel and is empowered by the Spirit: "And Gideon was clothed with the spirit of the LORD" (6:34). Yet before he leads his troops into battle, Gideon demands two more signs to assure himself that God will grant victory. He first asks that a woolen fleece he sets on the threshing floor become wet with dew while the floor around it remains dry. Then he asks that the same fleece remain dry while dew covers the floor around it (6:36-40). These signs are given, but they are still not enough for Gideon. So God suggests a fourth sign. Gideon is to go down to the enemy camp with his servant and listen to what is being said. When he does so, he hears an enemy soldier describing a dream. The soldier understands the dream as a sign that Gideon will be victorious (7:9-14). Gideon has now received assurance even from an enemy. He leads Israel into battle and defeats the enemy, initiating a period of peace that lasts forty years (8:28).

God is patient with Gideon's lack of confidence and his constant need for assurance. God knows Gideon is capable, but God is willing to wait until Gideon can recognize that truth himself.

Contemporary Relevance: At any time in our lives, God can call us to a new role or responsibility. The phone rings, and we realize that one of our children has developed a serious medical problem or that we have just become the primary caregiver for an aging parent. A dramatic shift occurs in our business, and we must assume a greater workload whether we are ready or not. Confronted with such demands, we may require significant assurance. Even if we, like Gideon, have significant resources at our disposal, such gifts do not necessarily negate the fear of failing or the questioning of our own abilities.

The story of Gideon reminds us that God is always willing to assure us. Even after God has called us and we have received the Spirit, we may still want further signs to boost our confidence. God is ready to provide them. The signs God provides will likely be less fanciful than Gideon's. We should not expect to see fire from the rock or dry wool on a floor drenched with dew. Instead our signs may be encouragement from a friend, a memory that gives us strength, or people and possibilities coming together in beautiful and unexpected ways. And once a sign is given, we are free to ask for another. God patiently waits as we express all our doubts and questions. God's Spirit continues to assure us until we are ready to act.

The Spirit and the Judges of Israel: Samson

Samson, whose story is narrated in Judges 13–16, is probably the best known of the judges. His great strength and wild exploits have fas-

Asking for a sign

The Scriptures do not always agree on the value of asking God for a sign. In most cases the request for a sign is seen as a positive way to faith, as in the story of Gideon (see also 2 Kgs 20:8-11; Isa 7:10-16). When Jesus' disciples ask for signs to determine the end of the age, he names several (Matt 24:3-30). However, other Scripture passages present the request for a sign negatively. Jesus says that an evil generation asks for a sign (Matt 12:38-39; 16:1-4; Mark 8:11-12; Luke 11:16, 29). In John's Gospel, though Jesus provides a variety of miraculous signs, his opponents continually ask him for more signs as proof of his claims (2:18; 6:30). These different perspectives on signs are difficult to reconcile. Part of any attempt, however, is the recognition that signs by nature are ambiguous. They can be sought for the wrong reason, as in the case of Herod wishing to see Jesus perform some sign (Luke 23:8). They can also originate from the wrong source, as in a sign from Satan (2 Thess 2:8-10).

cinated such diverse interpreters as John Milton and Cecil B. DeMille. Samson is the only one of Israel's judges to have a birth narrative in the Bible (see Judg 13). The angel who announces his birth commands that Samson live his life as a Nazirite (13:4-5). The word "Nazirite" comes from the Hebrew word *nazir*, meaning "to set apart as sacred."

Israelites could choose to be "set apart" for a sacred purpose by adopting the Nazirite practices enumerated in Numbers 6:1-8. These practices required Nazirites to abstain from wine or any product of the grapevine, to avoid contact with corpses (even the corpses of parents or siblings), and to never cut their hair. The Nazirite vow was usually made for a specific period of time. Samson is commanded to live his entire life as a Nazarite (13:7), setting him apart for the demanding role he will undertake as a judge. God is calling Samson to save Israel from assimilation into the surrounding culture, which was dominated at that time by the Philistines (13:1).

To enable his mission, Samson receives God's Spirit. No other judge is as frequently associated with this gift. As he grows up, the Spirit of the Lord comes upon him (13:24-25). When he is attacked by a lion, the Spirit provides him with strength: "But the spirit of the LORD rushed upon Samson, and he tore the lion apart barehanded, as one tears a young goat" (14:6). He is able to defeat thirty of his enemies because "[t]he spirit of the LORD rushed upon him" (14:19). When Samson, bound with ropes, is delivered to the Philistines, "the spirit of the LORD rushed upon him: the ropes around his arms became like flax that is consumed by fire, and his bonds melted away from his hands" (15:14).

God's Spirit is abundantly bestowed upon Samson. But the tragedy of his story is that the gift he receives is wasted. Though called as a judge for Israel, Samson spends his time pursuing his own interests. Unlike other judges, he never leads Israelite forces against an enemy. His conflicts with the Philistines are private in nature. One results from a wager he makes during his wedding (14:1-20). Another is connected to a dispute concerning his wife and another man (15:1-7). A third involves the attempt of some Judahites to hand him over (15:8-20).

Throughout his exploits, Samson consistently breaks his Nazirite vow. He visits vineyards (14:5) and arranges a seven-day wedding celebration at which wine was certainly served (14:10, 17). He not only has contact with the corpse of a lion but eats the honey he finds within it (14:8-9). He allows his hair to be cut (16:15-22). Most egregiously, Samson disregards the prohibition given at the beginning of the book of Judges: "you must not make a covenant with the inhabitants of this land" (2:2). Samson ignores this command completely. In fact, the plot of his story follows his desire to enter into relationships with three Philistine women: the Timnite (14:1–15:20), a prostitute from Gaza (16:1-3), and Delilah (16:4-31). Samson is controlled by his lust. When his parents question why he wants to marry "a woman from the uncircumcised Philistines," he cuts them short: "Get her for me, for she is the one I want" (14:3). Samson's whole life is directed by what he wants. This is hardly how one would expect a judge of Israel under a Nazirite vow to act.

Caught up in his sexual attractions and desire for revenge, Samson emerges as the worst of the judges. He breaks his vow. His life ends in self-destruction (16:23-30). Samson's story is a warning that God expects those who are chosen to cooperate with the gifts they have received. God's Spirit provides Samson with physical strength, but Samson is expected to use his strength for God's purposes. Because he is unwilling to do so, God's Spirit is wasted.

Contemporary Relevance: The sadness of Samson's story is not limited to the Bible. Most of us know individuals whose lives seem to be wasted. A person can be endowed with intelligence, energy, and an engaging personality and still be unsuccessful. A person can excel in college as a football star or class valedictorian only to go astray. Such decline is not fully explained by a lack of will or commitment. Poor choices, addiction, or the inability to recover from a tragedy are frequently factors of the deterioration, but the root cause often remains a mystery. Sometimes, as in the story of Samson, such lives end violently, with self-inflicted wounds.

We cannot explain such barren lives. We stand before them shaken, searching for hope. Here, the story of Samson provides a thin thread we may grasp. When Samson's hair is cut, he can no longer serve as a judge. His strength is taken away, and the Lord leaves him (16:20). The Philistines gouge out his eyes and bring him to a great celebration at the temple of the god Dagon to amuse the guests. Samson decides to end his life by pulling the temple down upon all those within it. To do this, he must regain his strength. So Samson cries out, "Lord GOD, remember me! Strengthen me only this once that I may avenge myself on the Philistines at one blow for my two eyes" (16:28). Samson has not changed. His request for strength is motivated, as usual, by his personal desire for vengeance. Yet he knows enough to turn to God. He asks for strength "only this once," which can also be translated "one last time." His prayer is the final request of a tragic life.

God hears Samson's prayer. God allows the worst of the judges to go out on his own terms. Moreover, although Samson's motivation is revenge, God uses his action for a larger purpose. Samson destroys the temple of Dagon—the god Samson was expected to confront had he been an effective judge. So as Samson dies fulfilling his own personal motives, he nevertheless strikes a blow for the God of Israel. Even when a promising life turns barren, God is free to bring good from within it. God's Spirit, which gives breath to every life, can still act in unexpected ways. Even when we cannot fathom the mystery of a life that seems wasted, the mystery of God's Spirit is greater.

The Spirit and the Kings of Israel: Saul and David

After the period of the judges, Israel moved toward a defined monarchy. Saul is a transitional figure in this development. His story is recounted in the book of First Samuel. The prophet Samuel anoints Saul as leader in 10:1, and Saul is proclaimed as king by the people in 10:24. The Spirit of God empowers Saul for his mission. After being anointed, Saul is told by Samuel that he will receive a sign that God is with him (10:2-8). The sign comes to pass in 10:10, when "a band of prophets met Saul, and the spirit of God rushed upon him, so that he joined them in their prophetic ecstasy." Later, when Nahash, the Ammonite, attacks Israel, the Spirit of God rushes upon Saul, who kills his oxen as a call to arms (11:6-7). Yet even with the gift of the Spirit, Saul's leadership in Israel is conflicted and unsuccessful. God ultimately rejects Saul as king (15:26).

A new leader must be found, and this leader will be David. He will become Israel's first true king, yet no one anticipates his selection. When God sends Samuel to Bethlehem, Samuel knows he is to anoint one of the sons of Jesse as king, but he has no idea which son it will be. The selection process is recounted below:

1 Samuel 16:4-13

Samuel Anoints David. [4]Samuel did as the LORD had commanded him. When he entered Bethlehem, the elders of the city came trembling to meet him and asked, "Is your visit peaceful, O seer?" [5]He replied: "Yes! I have come to sacrifice to the LORD. So purify yourselves and celebrate with me today." He also had Jesse and his sons purify themselves and invited them to the sacrifice. [6]As they came, he looked at Eliab and thought, "Surely the anointed is here before the LORD." [7]But the LORD said to Samuel: Do not judge from his appearance or from his lofty stature, because I have rejected him. God does not see as a mortal, who sees the appearance. The LORD looks into the heart. [8] Then Jesse called Abinadab and presented him before Samuel, who said, "The LORD has not chosen him." [9]Next Jesse presented Shammah, but Samuel said, "The LORD has not chosen this one either." [10]In the same way Jesse presented seven sons before Samuel, but Samuel said to Jesse, "The LORD has not chosen any one of these." [11]Then Samuel asked Jesse, "Are these all the sons you have?" Jesse replied, "There is still the youngest, but he is tending the sheep." Samuel said to Jesse, "Send for him; we will not sit down to eat until he arrives here." [12]Jesse had the young man brought to them. He was ruddy, a youth with beautiful eyes, and good looking. The LORD said: There—anoint him, for this is the one! [13]Then Samuel, with the horn of oil in hand, anointed him in the midst of his brothers, and from that day on, the spirit of the LORD rushed upon David. Then Samuel set out for Ramah.

Every society cultivates certain people to be leaders. Education, wealth, and physical prowess are the building blocks of the ruling class. When a vacancy occurs in the halls of power, it is to these selected few that people turn. They are the "beautiful people" who will be trusted with authority. Ancient Israel is no different. When Samuel is sent to Jesse's house, he expects to find noble candidates, and he is not disappointed. When the eldest son, Eliab, comes before him, he is impressed, thinking to himself, "Surely the anointed is here before the LORD" (v. 6). Eliab must have been a stunning man, an ideal candidate. Yet God tells Samuel that he is not the one. Although surprised, Samuel is not discouraged. There are six more strong candidates. But God rejects them, one by one (vv. 8-10).

At this point, the story comes to a standstill. There seems to be no way forward. All the expected choices have been rebuffed. With an air of desperation, Samuel asks Jesse, "Are these all the sons you have?" He seems to be pleading, "Have you perhaps left some handsome, ideal choice in the house?" Jesse's response is tinged with defeat: "There is still the youngest, but he is tending the sheep" (v. 11). Jesse admits there is one more son, but he clearly does

not consider him to be king material. When his sons were brought before Samuel, this youngest son did not make the cut. He was sent out into the field.

Then Samuel begins to understand. Although it runs contrary to every expectation, this youngest son could be God's choice. Although he had not been considered or prepared, it is possible that he is to be Israel's new king. Samuel demands that this last son be brought forward, and God's Spirit descends upon him. Only in this moment does the narrative reveal the youngest son's name. Up to this point, he has been both absent and without identity. Now, as the Spirit comes upon him, we hear the name of Israel's greatest king for the first time: "Then Samuel, with the horn of oil in hand, anointed him in the midst of his brothers, and from that day on, the spirit of the LORD rushed upon David" (v. 13).

Contemporary Relevance: We shape our world through our plans and expectations. We see how things work, and we try to find the pieces that will keep them working. We imagine who might facilitate the next communications breakthrough, discover a cure for cancer, or reconcile our polarized society. As positions are vacated, we turn to the expected candidates to fill them. Yet there are times when none of our choices seem viable. The story of David reminds us that God's Spirit is able to reach beyond our limited categories. Talent is present in those we never tried to prepare. Capability exists in those we never thought to consider. A person we would never think of as a leader can possess the exact resources that the situation requires. Such potential may have always been present, but we did not see it. That is why God sometimes prods us to look again.

God tells Samuel, "God does not see as a mortal, who sees the appearance. The LORD looks into the heart" (v. 7). This statement cannot mean that we are to disregard the way a person looks. When David comes forward, a great deal is made of his appearance: "He was ruddy, a youth with beautiful eyes, and good looking" (v. 12). Rather, this text is telling us that we must not limit our vision to what we have defined talent or beauty to be. We must not judge a person's abilities by the categories we have set up as desirable. A society is always richer when it searches for leaders outside the groups in which it expects to find them. Those without an Ivy League degree, six-figure income, or designer body might prove to be the Spirit's choice for the present need. And they are often beautiful. When David finally steps forward before Samuel, he is gorgeous. It is just that no one had ever looked at him before.

The Spirit and Balaam

As Israel came to the end of its wilderness journey, the twelve tribes approached the Promised Land. Their arrival caused concern among the inhabitants of the area. Moab was a kingdom east of the Dead Sea, and its king, Balak, was fearful that so numerous a people would harm the viability of his nation. Aware that his forces were too small to defeat Israel in battle, Balak adopted a nonmilitary strategy. He enlisted the services of a professional prophet to curse Israel and thus disrupt its settlement on the land. Such prophets, or seers, were commonly used in the Ancient Near East to assist kings in their responsibilities. The prophet employed by Balak was Balaam. He

was not from Moab, nor was he an Israelite. Balaam moved from one country to another practicing his trade. By all accounts, he was effective in his blessings and curses.

The story of Balak's attempts to curse Israel are found in the book of Numbers, chapters 22–24. When the envoys from Balak ask Balaam to accept the job, he is straightforward about the limits of his abilities. He knows that he can only speak what God directs him to speak (22:18). Nevertheless, Balaam agrees to go to Moab and see what is possible. Here, the story takes a comical turn. Three times Balaam is positioned to curse Israel, but each time he can only utter a blessing. Balak is present for all these attempts and shows growing frustration as the curses fail, one after the other.

In ancient thought, the one to be cursed should be in view in order for the curse to be effective. So, for the first attempt, Balak takes Balaam up to a high place from which Balaam could see part of the Israelite tribes and curse them (22:41). From that vantage point, Balaam blesses them instead (23:7-10). Thinking perhaps that the curse might work from another location, Balak then leads Balaam to a lookout post on the top of Pisgah (23:13-14). From there, Balaam blesses Israel again (23:18-24). Balak tries one last time. He brings Balaam to the top of Peor, where Balaam is given the best view of Israel yet (23:28). From this vantage

 ### What else do we know about Balaam?

In 1967, an inscription was discovered at Tell Deir Alla, on the east bank of the Jordan River, a flourishing city in the eighth and seventh centuries BCE. The inscription mentions Balaam, son of Beor, a seer who was possibly the same person as the biblical figure who was hired to curse the Israelites in Numbers 22–24. This discovery seems to confirm the fame of Balaam as a seer and possibly explains why Balak would be drawn to hire him to protect his country from the Israelites.

Although the presentation of Balaam in Numbers 22–24 is positive, other passages in the Bible that mention him are consistently negative. Deuteronomy 23:5-6, for example, claims that it was Balaam's intention to curse Israel (while in Num 22–24, Balaam insists that he will only speak what God wishes). Another negative claim about Balaam is made in Numbers 31:16. The New Testament continues the negative presentation, with 2 Peter 2:15-16 claiming Balaam loved doing wrong, and Jude 11 stating that he was consumed by personal gain (also see Rev 2:14).

Clearly there are two different traditions in Scripture concerning Balaam. In one, he is a foreign seer committed to God's will. In others, he is a false prophet determined to curse Israel.

point, Balaam blesses Israel a third time (24:3-9). Not surprisingly, Balak erupts in "a blaze of anger." Clapping his hands (a sign of contempt or derision), he says to Balaam, "It was to lay a curse on my foes that I summoned you here; yet three times now you have actually blessed them!" (24:10). Balak sends Balaam away without paying him. He feels cheated. He hired the seer for a curse, but Balaam only uttered blessings. As Balaam leaves for his own country, he offers a fourth blessing of Israel for good measure!

As we look back over the narrative, we can see that as Balak's frustration grew, a change was also taking place in Balaam. The seer shifts his attitude and practice after the first two blessings: "Balaam, however, perceiving that the LORD was pleased to bless Israel, did not go aside as before to seek omens, but turned his gaze toward the wilderness. When Balaam looked up and saw Israel encamped, tribe by tribe, the spirit of God came upon him" (24:1-2).

The change in Balaam is caused by the Spirit of God. In the first two blessings, Balaam is directed externally by God's commands. He can only speak as God allows him to speak. He cannot curse "one whom God has not cursed" (23:8). He must bless because God demands it (23:20). But after the Spirit comes upon him, Balaam is guided by an internal authority. Balaam begins both the third and fourth blessings by asserting his closeness to God: "The oracle of one who hears what God says, / and knows what the Most High knows, / Of one who sees what the Almighty sees, / in rapture and with eyes unveiled" (24:4, 16). Balaam no longer requires guidance from external sources. Now God's Spirit within him allows him to know what God knows and to see what God sees. He speaks in the rapture of the Spirit "with eyes unveiled." Balaam initially agreed to prophesy because he was hired by Balak. It was his job. But he ends up deeply changed, delivering blessings that flow spontaneously from his union with God's Spirit.

Contemporary Relevance: Balaam's experience resonates with us. We often assume roles with a specific need or goal in mind. Over time,

Balaam blessing Israel

these roles may grow into something more. We meet someone at school and begin to socialize. We enjoy each other's company, and the relationship grows. In time that person becomes a confidant and lifelong friend, a significant gift of God. Or perhaps we become a single parent. We take up that role as a necessary task and push through its multiple challenges. But as the years pass, we discover that the bonds within our family have not only changed but deepened. In a way we had not anticipated, our children are now a concrete manifestation of God's care for us. Or maybe we work a few days in a hunger center as a Lenten penance. It just seems the right thing to do. But as we meet people and hear their stories, we come to see that we are receiving more than we have given. Our service has become a blessing for us.

There are many ways God can change us, but few are as beautiful as the way God changed Balaam. We know that the Spirit of God is with us when a responsibility becomes a vocation, an acquaintance becomes a life-giving friend, or a task becomes a gift of love.

The Spirit and Joseph

The story of Joseph differs from the narratives of the other patriarchs in the book of Genesis. The traditions regarding Abraham, Isaac, and Jacob occur in small, discrete scenes, seldom extending beyond twenty verses. But the story of Joseph is a lengthy, well-crafted narrative covering fourteen chapters (37–50). Its form is that of a small novel, containing multiple scenes and plot developments.

Joseph clearly possesses God's Spirit. In the midst of his story, Joseph finds himself in the Egyptian court, where he interprets Pharaoh's dreams. As a reward for his service, Pharaoh elevates Joseph to rule Egypt as his second-in-command. Pharaoh explains his reasoning to his servants: "Could we find another like him, . . . a man so endowed with the spirit of God?" (41:38). This is the first time in the Bible that any character is said to possess God's Spirit.

The fact that the Spirit is only mentioned once in the fourteen chapters of the Joseph story does not lessen its importance. The narrative is written in a notably "secular" manner. With the exception of a visionary assurance in Genesis 46:2-4, there are no divine apparitions or communications within it. God's Spirit is active but concealed, working behind the scenes. Ishmaelite traders pass by at the right time (37:28). Pharaoh has a dream he cannot understand (41:8). A royal cupbearer remembers that Joseph can interpret dreams (41:9-13). The need for food draws Joseph's brothers into his presence (42:1-5). It is only as the story ends that the characters realize God has been at work. Once they are reunited, Joseph tells his brothers, "But now do not be distressed, and do not be angry with yourselves for having

sold me here. It was really for the sake of saving lives that *God sent me here* ahead of you" (45:5; emphasis added). The Spirit of God works in many ways within the Joseph narrative. Here, will focus on one of them: the Spirit as an agent of reconciliation.

The story of Joseph is, among other things, a story about the healing of a family. Jacob (or Israel, as he is sometimes called in Scripture) has twelve sons, but his family is divided by favoritism. Genesis 37:3-8 does not hide Jacob's (Israel's) preference for Joseph:

Genesis 37:3-8

[3]Israel loved Joseph best of all his sons, for he was the child of his old age; and he had made him a long ornamented tunic. [4]When his brothers saw that their father loved him best of all his brothers, they hated him so much that they could not say a kind word to him.

[5]Once Joseph had a dream, and when he told his brothers, they hated him even more. [6]He said to them, "Listen to this dream I had. [7]There we were, binding sheaves in the field, when suddenly my sheaf rose to an upright position, and your sheaves formed a ring around my sheaf and bowed down to it." [8]His brothers said to him, "Are you really going to make yourself king over us? Will you rule over us?" So they hated him all the more because of his dreams and his reports.

Three times in the above passage, Joseph's brothers are said to hate him. Their hatred leads to violence: the brothers decide to kill Joseph (37:18-20). Judah prevents his death by persuading the other brothers to sell Joseph as a slave to some Ishmaelite traders, who carry him off to Egypt (37:25-28). To hide their treachery, the brothers tell Jacob that Joseph has been killed by a wild beast. Jacob resolves to mourn his favorite son until his dying day (37:32-35). The family has been broken. Joseph has been enslaved. The brothers have blood on their hands. Jacob has assumed a permanent state of grief.

The patriarch Jacob had twelve sons, but they did not share the same mother. The patriarchal narratives accept the presence of multiple wives within the family. Moreover, in cases where children were not conceived in a marriage, it was permissible for the patriarch to have children with his wife's maid. Jacob had two wives: Leah and Rachel. Rueben, Levi, Simeon, and Judah were sons of Jacob and Leah. Gad and Asher were sons of Jacob and Leah's maidservant, Zilpah. Dan and Naphtali were sons of Jacob and Rachel's maidservant, Bilhah. Joseph and Benjamin were children of Jacob and Rachel. From the start, Jacob loved Rachel more than Leah. So, it is not surprising that Joseph and Benjamin were his favorite children. The story of **the building of Jacob's line** is recounted in Genesis 29–30.

Joseph's story could have ended here, with a family destroyed by favoritism, jealousy, hatred, and violence. But God's Spirit is active, and the story continues. Many years pass. Joseph does not languish in Egypt but rises to a position second only to Pharaoh. Joseph marries Asenath, an Egyptian woman, and has two sons, Manasseh and Ephraim (41:50-52). Joseph is an Egyptian now. It seems that his broken family in the land of Canaan has been forgotten.

Then there is a famine. Egypt has grain, and Joseph, as Pharaoh's governor, controls it. Far away, in the land of Canaan, the family of Jacob is desperate for food. Ten of Joseph's brothers travel to Egypt to buy grain. Joseph is not on their minds, as they presume he is dead. When they are brought before the governor, they do not recognize him. Joseph, however, recognizes them. Here, the text offers important information: "When Joseph recognized his brothers, although they did not recognize him, he was reminded of the dreams he had about them" (42:8-9). The text reveals that Joseph has been dreaming. The dreams certainly include the dreams he had in Canaan that so infuriated his brothers. But they may also include the dreams he has had in Egypt, perhaps waking from them in the night, nurturing wounds from the brothers who betrayed him and longing for the father who so loved him. Although it seemed that Joseph had forgotten his family, the narrative reveals that his painful past has been haunting his sleep.

Those who caused that painful past now stand before Joseph, asking for food. His brothers once had all the power, but now Joseph has complete authority over them. What will Joseph do? In an act of trickery, Joseph accuses them of being spies (42:9), a charge which forces the brothers to defend themselves. They tell their story: "We your servants . . . are twelve brothers, sons of a certain man in Canaan; but the youngest one is at present with our father, and the other one is no more" (42:13). Although Joseph's brothers believe he "is no more," they cannot define themselves without including him. It has been many years since they betrayed him, but he is still a member of their broken family. It is clear that the memory of Joseph and their violence toward him remains fixed in their minds. Neither Joseph nor his brothers are free from the painful actions of the past.

The youngest of the brothers, Benjamin, is still with Jacob in Canaan. He is especially close to Joseph since the two of them have the same mother, Rachel. Motivated by that closeness, Joseph insists that one brother, Simeon, must remain in Egypt until Benjamin is brought to him (42:18-20). This request stirs up the brothers' guilt in betraying Joseph: "Truly we are being punished because of our brother. We saw the anguish of his heart when he pleaded with us, yet we would not listen. That is why this anguish has now come upon us" (42:21). Not only do Joseph's brothers remember him as a part of their family, but the guilt of betraying him also burns within them.

The brokenness of Jacob's family is on full display. Simeon is held captive in Egypt.

Joseph mourns his separation from Benjamin and his loving father. The nine brothers return home, remembering their sin against Joseph and aware that they can never return to Egypt without Benjamin. Jacob continues lamenting Joseph, his lost son, and is determined never to let Benjamin go.

Here, the story seems to end again. But God's Spirit is still active. The famine continues. Jacob is forced to send his sons to Egypt a second time. He allows Benjamin to go with them only when Judah vows that he will not return home without him (43:1-10). When Joseph sees Benjamin, he is so overcome with emotion that he must leave the room to weep (43:29-30). Joseph then constructs a test for his brothers, to see if they have learned anything in the years since they betrayed him. He insists that Benjamin remain with him (44:1-17). Joseph wants to see whether his brothers will abandon Benjamin as they once abandoned him. The test is not how much the brothers love Benjamin but how much they love their father. Can they now accept their father's favoritism toward Benjamin even though they could not tolerate it when it was directed toward Joseph? The tension builds as Judah steps forward to speak. He offers the longest speech in Genesis and one of the most beautiful in the Bible. This is how it ends:

Genesis 44:30-34

[30]"So now, if the boy is not with us when I go back to your servant my father, whose very life is bound up with his, he will die as soon as he sees that the boy is missing; [31]and your servants will thus send the white head of your servant our father down to Sheol in grief. [32]Besides, I, your servant, have guaranteed the boy's safety for my father by saying, 'If I fail to bring him back to you, father, I will bear the blame before you forever.' [33]So now let me, your servant, remain in place of the boy as the slave of my lord, and let the boy go back with his brothers. [34]How could I go back to my father if the boy were not with me? I could not bear to see the anguish that would overcome my father."

Judah is willing to give his life for the sake of his doting father. He who sold his brother into slavery is willing to become the slave of the one who was sold. Judah has passed the test. His love inspires Joseph to reveal himself: "I am Joseph. . . . Is my father still alive?" (45:3). Judah's love for his father allows Joseph to express his love for his father. In that love, Judah and Joseph are brothers again. Judah's sacrifice permits the curse of the past to be broken. It allows wounds to mend and guilt to dissipate. A father will soon be able to hold his lost son once more. All the obstacles of favoritism, jealousy, violence, remorse, and grief begin to fall like a house of cards. The healing of Jacob's family has begun.

Contemporary Relevance: The Spirit of God moves through the Joseph narrative to bring about reconciliation. Here are two ways this story speaks to reconciliation in our lives.

1) *People can change.* The story of Joseph turns on the ability of Judah to change. He once instigated the enslavement of his brother. Now, when he faces the enslavement of Benjamin and the heartbreak of his father, he offers to take Benjamin's place. Judah's change precipitates a change in Joseph and allows the family to be reunited. When our families are broken because of the actions of members within them, it is easy to presume that people will always stay the same. Those who were jealous before will be jealous again. Those who did not think of others will continue to think only of themselves. But the story of Joseph asserts that change is possible.

Why was Judah able to change? For the same reason that change takes place in us. God's Spirit works through our experiences. As time passes, we mature beyond the childish actions of our youth. We experience more of life. We have children, and they call us to a greater and more flexible love. We experience loss and come to realize how fragile relationships are. We make mistakes and must face our imperfections. We count our blessings and realize that life is too short for grudges. The experiences of Judah allow him to change.

When he is put to the test, he does not repeat the mistakes of the past. Life is able to transform us into better people. When such growth occurs, God's Spirit is at work.

2) *God works in hidden ways.* We discussed at the beginning of this section how the Joseph story was written in a secular manner. God's Spirit is clearly active but works "behind the scenes." The Spirit works in a similar way in our lives. Few of us receive a visit from an angel or witness the heavens torn open. God more often leads us through quiet promptings, ideas that come to us, friends who guide us, and life events that give us pause. Just as God led the brothers to Egypt because of a famine, God can direct us by the trials we endure. Just as Joseph's brothers recalled their guilt as they told their story, God can stir memories of our past mistakes so we can repent and address them. Like Joseph, we might not recognize God's action until our story draws to an end. But that is what makes the Joseph narrative so valuable. It shows us that even when God's plan is not obvious, God's Spirit is still moving, drawing the broken pieces of our lives toward repentance and reconciliation.

Joseph reveals himself to his brothers, 1870 engraving by Gustave Dore

EXPLORING LESSON TWO

1. Exodus 31:1-6 connects the making of beautiful things by human artists with the Spirit's act of creation. Has the impact of a painting, drama, dance, song, or other artistic creation ever led you closer to God? In what way?

_____

_____

_____

_____

_____

_____

2. Who were the judges of Israel? What pattern repeats itself in the book of Judges? Does this pattern speak in any way to your own relationship with God?

_____

_____

_____

_____

_____

3. God is presented as being patient with Gideon, waiting for him to recognize the power of God's Spirit within him. Can you identify times in your own life when you knew God was being patient with you? What was God waiting for you to recognize?

_____

_____

_____

_____

_____

4. What was the Nazirite vow in ancient Israel? How does Samson's fidelity to this vow affect his relationship with God in the book of Judges?

_____

_____

_____

_____

_____

5. The commentary suggests that Samson wastes the gift of God's Spirit that is given to him. Have you known people whose lives seem to be wasted? Does the story of Samson provide you with some basis of hope or a different perspective? Why or why not?

_____

_____

_____

_____

_____

_____

6. The story of David being chosen as king purposely presents him as an overlooked candidate for leadership (1 Sam 16:4-13). What people or groups do you feel are overlooked in our society today? In your opinion, what leads us to narrow our appreciation of beauty or talent?

_____

_____

_____

_____

_____

7. Describe the way the Spirit of God changes Balaam in Numbers 22–24. Can you remember a similar change occurring in your life? What has been the result of that change?

_____

_____

_____

_____

8. In what way is the family of Jacob divided by favoritism and rivalry in the story of Joseph? Does it support or frustrate your faith to realize that such a central family of Israel was so wounded? In what way?

_____

_____

_____

_____

9. The story of Joseph is described as a "secular narrative" in which the actions of God are not described or recognized until the ending. Have there been times in your life when it seemed that God was not present, but looking back, you can see how God was leading, guiding, and shaping you?

_____

_____

_____

_____

_____

_____

_____

CLOSING PRAYER

Prayer

Then Samuel, with the horn of oil in hand, anointed him in the midst of his brothers, and from that day on, the spirit of the Lord rushed upon David. (1 Sam 16:13)

Lord our God, your Spirit is active in human history. You have shaped the lives of your people through the ages, and you continue to shape our lives today. Help us to be attentive to your presence—to sense when you are near and to know when you are with us. Equip us to create, to lead, to bless, to reconcile, and to do whatever good work you have planned for us. Today we pray especially for those in our own communities who are called to leadership, that your Spirit may be with them, especially . . .

LESSON THREE

The Holy Spirit and the People of Israel

Begin your personal study and group discussion with a simple and sincere prayer such as:

Prayer

Spirit of God, you breathe life into human beings and into your Word. Fill us with your presence as we spend time with your Word and one another. Re-create us and sustain us day by day.

Read pages 46–56, Lesson Three.

Respond to the questions on pages 57–59, Exploring Lesson Three.

The Closing Prayer on page 59 is for your personal use and may be used at the end of group discussion.

THE HOLY SPIRIT AND
THE PEOPLE OF ISRAEL

In biblical history, Israel's most profound crisis was the exile. The monarchy established by David came to an end in 587 BCE as the Babylonian ruler Nebuchadrezzar devastated Jerusalem and destroyed Solomon's temple. Jews were scattered. The most influential exiles were taken to Babylon, where they remained until 539 BCE. Even after the Persian king Cyrus permitted the exiles to return to what was left of Jerusalem, the Jews were never again free from foreign domination.

The exile was a political disaster. But it was during this period that the Jewish faith began to expand in new directions. Without a king as a focus for religious and political life, Israel had to imagine its relationship to God in new ways. These developments influenced the understanding of God's Spirit. In biblical texts that describe life before the exile, the Spirit is given to individuals (see Lesson Two). But during the exile, Israel begins to experience and understand the Spirit as the animating force of the entire people. This lesson will trace the emergence of this new awareness in the oracles of Ezekiel and Joel. It will also examine how Israel begins to envision a new world order that will be directed by a leader imbued with the Spirit of God.

The word **"oracle"** derives from a Latin root meaning "to pray" and refers to speech in relationship to God. In the ancient world, priests or priestesses who acted as mediums through whom advice or prophecy was sought from the gods were known as "oracles." The term also referred to the content of the advice or prophecy. "Oracle" is used in this sense in relation to the prophets of the Bible. Their words or oracles were understood as being spoken in God's name.

The Spirit Re-Creates a People

The prophet Ezekiel was active among the exiles in Babylon. His oracles interpret the exile as God's punishment for the people's unfaithfulness. But they also announce that God will create a new Israel able to follow God's will. The most famous of these oracles is Ezekiel 37:1-14, in which the prophet is led into a valley of dry bones. The Spirit plays a major role in what unfolds:

Ezekiel 37:1-14

Vision of the Dry Bones. [1]The hand of the LORD came upon me, and he led me out in the spirit of the LORD and set me in the center of the broad valley. It was filled with bones. [2]He made me walk among them in every direction. So many lay on the surface of the valley! How dry they were! [3]He asked me: Son of man, can these bones come back to life? "Lord GOD," I answered, "you alone know that." [4]Then he said to me: Prophesy over these bones, and say to them: Dry bones, hear the word of the LORD! [5]Thus says the Lord GOD to these bones: Listen! I will make breath enter you so you may come to life. [6]I will put sinews on you, make flesh grow over you, cover you with skin, and put breath into you so you may come to life. Then you shall know that I am the LORD. ⁷I prophesied as I had been commanded. A sound started up, as I was prophesying, rattling like thunder. The bones came together, bone joining to bone. ⁸As I watched, sinews appeared on them, flesh grew over them, skin covered them on top, but there was no breath in them. ⁹Then he said to me: Prophesy to the breath, prophesy, son of man! Say to the breath: Thus says the Lord GOD: From the four winds come, O breath, and breathe into these slain that they may come to life. ¹⁰I prophesied as he commanded me, and the breath entered them; they came to life and stood on their feet, a vast army. ¹¹He said to me: Son of man, these bones are the whole house of Israel! They are saying, "Our bones are dried up, our hope is lost, and we are cut off." ¹²Therefore, prophesy and say to them: Thus says the Lord GOD: Look! I am going to open your graves; I will make you come up out of your graves, my people, and bring you back to the land of Israel. ¹³You shall know that I am the LORD, when I open your graves and make you come up out of them, my people! ¹⁴I will put my spirit in you that you may come to life, and I will settle you in your land. Then you shall know that I am the LORD. I have spoken; I will do it—oracle of the LORD.

There are two parts to this passage. Verses 1-10 present the vision given to Ezekiel, and verses 11-14 interpret the vision. The vision is one of total death. Ezekiel sees a broad valley filled with bones. They are not skeletons but a vast display of disjointed bones, randomly scattered. Any semblance of a human shape was lost long ago. The bones, picked clean by the birds of the air, are the last remnants of previous life. To ensure the full impact of the scene, God leads the prophet back and forth around the bones (v. 2). Ezekiel sees firsthand how many and how dry they are. In this valley, death reigns in horror and finality.

Then God asks Ezekiel what seems like a ridiculous question: "[C]an these bones come back to life?" The prophet responds, "Lord GOD, . . . you alone know that" (v. 3). Although Ezekiel's response may seem to avoid God's question, it points to the central message of the passage. If these bones are to come back to life, it will not be by any human power. God alone can make such bones live. And God will do so through the Spirit.

The Hebrew word *ruach* saturates this passage, occurring ten times in fourteen verses. The NABRE translation above renders it as "spirit" (vv. 1 and 14), "breath" (vv. 5, 6, 8, 9 [three times], and 10), and "wind" (v. 9). The word occurs most frequently in verses 4-10 as God brings the dry bones to life. God commands Ezekiel to prophesy to the bones. When he does, he hears a rattling like thunder. It is the sound of bones coming together, each to its proper place (v. 7). The rattling bones are soon covered with sinews, flesh, and skin. Then the action stops. These reassembled bodies have "no breath in them" (v. 8). Ezekiel must prophesy again for breath to enter them so that they may live.

The gift of God's breath in this passage is modeled on the creation of the first human in Genesis 2:7. In both Genesis and Ezekiel, God's work takes place in two steps. God first forms the human person (out of dust from the ground or out of dry bones) and then breathes into the creature the breath of life. It is not until God's *ruach* enters the human forms that they become living beings. Only the Creator of all can make dust and dry bones live, and only through the power of God's own breath (v. 10).

Verses 11-14 interpret the vision. The dry bones are the whole house of Israel. The people languish in exile, feeling abandoned by God, as dead as dry bones (v. 11). But in this moment of complete despair, God promises to re-create them. They will live again, and the animating force will be the Spirit. The breath of God will enter them (v. 10), the breath of God's own Spirit (v. 14). This is a key change of perspective occasioned by the exile. The Spirit of God, once understood as the possession of select individuals, now animates the entire people.

The book of Ezekiel identifies its author as "the priest Ezekiel, the son of Buzi" (1:3). This indicates that **Ezekiel once served as a priest** in the temple of Jerusalem. When the city was destroyed and he was carried off with the other exiles to Babylon, Ezekiel could no longer offer sacrifices in the temple. Priestly concerns, however, characterize the book that bears his name. The priest's role is to maintain the purity of the community because of God's presence in its midst. Even as Ezekiel insists that the people have been defiled by their sins, he announces that God will make them holy and capable of following God's will.

Contemporary Relevance: The vision Ezekiel receives in 37:1-14 asserts that God can accomplish what seems impossible to us. Because God is Creator, God can make dry bones live.

1) *God does the impossible through us.* Except for one statement by the prophet in verse 3, all of Ezekiel 37:1-14 is spoken by God. The prophet is entirely subordinated to God's voice. Yet Ezekiel still has a role to play in God's action. He is directed by God to prophesy that the dry bones come together (vv. 4-8). He is commanded to speak to the breath, that it might bring those slain to life (vv. 9-10). Finally, he is to prophesy to the people that they may understand the vision (vv. 11-14). Re-creation is the work of God, but God involves Ezekiel in its execution.

We at times encounter situations that seem utterly hopeless. We may know parents who are devastated by the death of an infant, a family member ruined by addiction, or a friend sexually abused and now unable to maintain loving relationships. These are the dry bones of our lives. We understand that only God's grace can turn such death into life. But Ezekiel 37:1-14 reminds us that when God undertakes the work of re-creation, we may be asked to play a part. Like the prophet, we may be commanded to speak to dry bones. We may be summoned to offer hope time and again even when it seems foolish to do so. We may be directed to suggest that new life is possible even when it appears to be wishful thinking. We are not God. We cannot infuse new life. But we can testify to a God who can, even in the valley of death, and we can serve as God's instruments as new life unfolds. God may use our voices to cry out: "Dry bones, hear the word of the LORD!" (v. 4).

2) *The Spirit can unravel what we have bound up.* Although verse 9 indicates that the dry bones belonged to those who were slain, the killing is not described. However, once these human beings lost the breath of life, we can easily imagine the process of decay that followed. The corpses began to deteriorate in stages: first the skin, then the muscle, until all that remained were bones. Then, the bones themselves were separated and scattered. In Ezekiel 37:1-14 the re-creation by God takes place in reverse order. First the bones reconnect (v. 7). Then, sinews, flesh, and skin appear (v. 8). Finally, breath is given so that the assembled parts may live (v. 10). Dying and deterioration take place in successive steps. God's re-creation reverses them, one by one.

This aspect of the text speaks to complex problems in our culture. Every society is shaped by ideas, movements, and priorities that either advance or detract from its viability. Commercialism, individualism, sexism, and racism are but a few examples of forces that draw societies toward death. Such structures are resilient, resulting from long histories of development. Consider racism. Decades of economic, moral, and political choices constructed the edifice of slavery. And although slavery has ended, the societal and individual attitudes that enabled its existence continue to influence us. Racism is a tightly bound knot tied into the fabric of American life. It may seem hopeless that such an enmeshed structure could ever be undone.

This passage from Ezekiel shows us that God's Spirit is capable of unraveling what we have bound together. Working through women and men of good will, the Spirit can unwind the compounded layers of racism. God's Spirit can open our eyes and breathe into our hearts the love and courage to act so that the stereotypes and structures of racism are disassembled. No problem is too complex for the Spirit to heal.

Death imposes its control through a gradual process of deterioration, but God's Spirit can bring our wounded culture back to life, step by step.

The Spirit and Israel's Prophets

The Bible presents the Spirit as God's power to judges, kings, and the early prophets such as Elijah (2 Kgs 2:9). After the exile, the Spirit is again shown to enable the work of prophets such as Ezekiel (2:2) and Zechariah (4:6). In most of the prophetic books, however, prophets are seldom explicitly said to be inspired by the Spirit. Instead, their connection to God is through "the word of the LORD" (Isa 38:4; Jer 1:2; Hos 1:1; Amos 7:16; Mic 1:1; Zeph 1:1). Although there are exceptions to this practice (see, for example, Hos 9:7; Mic 3:8), this focus on God's word clearly emphasizes the importance of the prophet delivering God's message.

The Spirit Gives a New Heart

Ezekiel 36:16-38 further expands our understanding of God's Spirit as given to the people of Israel. The first section of this oracle reads as follows:

Ezekiel 36:16-28

Regeneration of the People. [16]The word of the LORD came to me: [17]Son of man, when the house of Israel lived in its land, they defiled it with their behavior and their deeds. In my sight their behavior was like the impurity of a woman in menstruation. [18]So I poured out my fury upon them for the blood they poured out on the ground and for the idols with which they defiled it. [19]I scattered them among the nations, and they were dispersed through other lands; according to their behavior and their deeds I carried out judgment against them. [20]But when they came to the nations, where they went, they desecrated my holy name, for people said of them: "These are the people of the LORD, yet they had to leave their land." [21]So I relented because of my holy name which the house of Israel desecrated among the nations to which they came. [22]Therefore say to the house of Israel: Thus says the Lord GOD: Not for your sake do I act, house of Israel, but for the sake of my holy name, which you desecrated among the nations to which you came. [23]But I will show the holiness of my great name, desecrated among the nations, in whose midst you desecrated it. Then the nations shall know that I am the LORD—oracle of the Lord GOD—when through you I show my holiness before their very eyes. [24]I will take you away from among the nations, gather you from all the lands, and bring you back to your own soil. [25]I will sprinkle clean water over you to make you clean; from all your impurities and from all your idols I will cleanse you. [26]I will give you a new heart, and a new spirit I will put within you. I will remove the heart of stone from your flesh and give you a heart of flesh. [27]I will put my spirit within you so that you walk in my statutes, observe my ordinances, and keep them. [28]You will live in the land I gave to your ancestors; you will be my people, and I will be your God.

This passage is similar to the vision of the dry bones in Ezekiel 37. In both passages God re-creates Israel. But in Ezekiel 36, God's actions are viewed through a moral lens. Verses 16-19 present Ezekiel's prophetic understanding of why the exile happened: Israel had defiled the land with sinful deeds and was therefore scattered among the nations. Now, however, God intends to deal with Israel's sinfulness. First God will sprinkle clean water for cleansing (v. 25). Then God will give to the house of Israel "a new heart, and a new spirit," which will be God's own Spirit (vv. 26-27). This Spirit will enable Israel to do God's will. Not only will God's people be forgiven, but they will be given the means to avoid sin and to live faithfully in the future.

Ezekiel's promise of a new heart is likely influenced by the prophet Jeremiah's promise of a new covenant:

Jeremiah 31:31-34

The New Covenant. [31]See, days are coming—oracle of the LORD—when I will make a new covenant with the house of Israel and the house of Judah. [32]It will not be like the covenant I made with their ancestors the day I took them by the hand to lead them out of the land of Egypt. They broke my covenant, though I was their master—oracle of the LORD. [33]But this is the covenant I will make with the house of Israel after those days—oracle of the LORD. I will place my law within them, and write it upon their hearts; I will be their God, and they shall be my people. [34]They will no longer teach their friends and relatives, "Know the LORD!" Everyone, from least to greatest, shall know me—oracle of the LORD—for I will forgive their iniquity and no longer remember their sin.

Jeremiah's announcement that God will write the law upon the people's hearts and Ezekiel's promise of the gift of a new heart pull in the same direction. Both enable the people to do God's will. God gives Israel a new heart so that a new covenant, a new relationship, may exist. Israel will be able to do what is right. A passage earlier in Ezekiel confirms this perspective: "And I will give them another heart and a new spirit I will put within them. From their bodies I will remove the hearts of stone, and give them hearts of flesh, so that they walk according to my statutes, taking care to keep my ordinances. Thus they will be my people, and I will be their God" (11:19-20).

A new heart is given so that Israel can obey God. But this focus on obedience is not an end in itself. Obedience to God makes a relationship with God possible. All three of the passages just cited make this explicit. The purpose of the new heart is that "you will be my people,

and I will be your God" (Ezek 36:28; see Jer 31:33; Ezek 11:20). The heart that allows that new relationship is the gift of God's Spirit.

 The **"new covenant"** that Jeremiah announces in 31:31-34 does not replace the divine teaching of the Jewish law. It instills it into human hearts. This is why no one will need to teach another to know the Lord. God's truth and presence are already within God's people. This limitless grace has led Christians to associate the new covenant with Jesus' life, death, and resurrection. At the Last Supper, Jesus takes the cup and says, "This cup is the new covenant in my blood, which will be shed for you" (Luke 22:20).

Ezekiel is convinced that before the exile, Israel was incapable of doing what God desired. Israel's disobedience led to exile and death. But when God re-creates Israel through the Spirit, Israel will receive the capacity to be faithful. This new relationship in the Spirit is final and irrevocable. Ezekiel uses a remarkable image to assert this conviction: "I will no longer hide my face from them once I pour out my spirit upon the house of Israel—oracle of the Lord GOD" (39:29). Here Ezekiel no longer speaks of "putting the Spirit within." Now the Spirit is "poured out," suggesting that the Spirit is like a liquid that "fills up" Israel, suffusing the people with new life. Formerly Israel was unable to do God's will. Now the life of the Spirit saturates the people. Israel is God's forever.

Another aspect of Ezekiel 36:16-28 deserves consideration. Ezekiel has insisted that God, who scattered Israel because of disobedience, now forgives and re-creates the people. But why does God forgive and re-create? Ezekiel has a definitive answer: "Thus says the Lord GOD: Not for your sake do I act, house of Israel, but for the sake of my holy name, which you desecrated among the nations to which you came" (v. 22). According to Ezekiel, God gives Israel a new heart not for Israel's sake but for *God's* sake. God insists that the divine name is being sullied by association with a people who are scattered because of their sins. Other nations see Israel's situation and conclude that Israel's God does not have the power to protect them (36:20). Exile in Babylon is ruining God's reputation. Therefore, God decides to forgive and re-create Israel to forestall any further embarrassment and to create a people worthy of God's name.

Contemporary Relevance: Ezekiel's stated reason for God's forgiveness runs counter to our usual understanding. We believe that God forgives out of love for us. Rightly so. Many passages in both the Hebrew Scriptures and the New Testament affirm that love is God's motivation for mercy. Yet Ezekiel provides another perspective. Insisting that God forgives us for God's sake allows Ezekiel to emphasize two important spiritual realities.

The first concerns the scandal of sinfulness. When we sin, we assume that our failures reflect poorly on us. Ezekiel reminds us that they also reflect poorly on God. As people of faith, we are connected to God, and others know it. When we lie, manipulate, seek revenge, or promote violence, God's name is tarnished by our failures. Others rightly shake their heads, look at the damage we have caused, and say with cynicism, "And she claims to be a Christian" or "He is such a hypocrite." There is no doubt that our sins hurt us, but they also diminish God in the eyes of others and make faith in God less credible.

Second, Ezekiel's approach short-circuits our attempts to be worthy of God's mercy. Forgiveness is always God's free gift. Yet we are tempted to connect God's mercy to some remnant of our own goodness. We do this through excuses: "I was tempted on a bad day" or "I was only trying to help" or "I was so overwhelmed that I just reacted." Such excuses suggest that God should forgive us because there were extenuating circumstances. Our sin was not so bad.

But such thinking is dangerous, and not only because it seeks to justify our sinful behavior. What happens when we sin so deeply that we can find no excuse, when our failures are so destructive that we know any defense is meaningless? In those circumstances, we can find no reason why God would ever forgive us. Ezekiel reminds us that the reason for God's forgiveness is not to be found in any shred of *our* worthiness. It is to be found in God's own self. God freely chooses to forgive us, even if we have no goodness to claim as our own. God re-creates us in the Spirit for the glory of God's own name.

The Spirit Ensures Inclusiveness and Dignity

We do not know with certainty when the book of Joel was written. Internal evidence, however, favors a date after the exile. One indicator of this is Joel's familiarity with Ezekiel. Like Ezekiel, Joel envisions a "pouring out" of God's Spirit upon the people:

Joel 3:1-5

The Day of the Lord. ¹It shall come to pass
I will pour out my spirit upon all flesh.
Your sons and daughters will prophesy,
your old men will dream dreams,
your young men will see visions.
²Even upon your male and female servants,
in those days, I will pour out my spirit.
³I will set signs in the heavens and on the earth,
blood, fire, and columns of smoke;
⁴The sun will darken,
the moon turn blood-red,
Before the day of the LORD arrives,
that great and terrible day.
⁵Then everyone who calls upon the name of the LORD
will escape harm.
For on Mount Zion there will be a remnant,
as the LORD has said,
And in Jerusalem survivors
whom the LORD will summon.

The pouring out of the Spirit is mentioned twice in this passage (vv. 1-2). As in Ezekiel, the Spirit will be given lavishly, and the people will be filled up with God's presence. Ezekiel connected this generous outpouring to a new heart, one able to obey God's will. Other biblical authors, however, have associated the outpouring of the Spirit with different aspects of God's design for the world. In Zechariah 12:10, the Spirit is given as a gift of mercy: "I will pour out on the house of David and on the inhabitants of Jerusalem a spirit of mercy and supplication, so that when they look on him whom they have thrust through, they will mourn for him as one mourns for an only child, and they will grieve for him as one grieves over a firstborn." Isaiah 32:15 promises that the pouring out of the Spirit will rejuvenate despoiled nature: "Until the spirit from on high / is poured out on us. / And the wilderness becomes a garden land / and the garden land seems as common as forest."

The prophet Joel uses the outpouring of the Spirit to announce another result: an inclusive community. Joel connects the Spirit to prophecy, dreams, and visions (v. 1). Such gifts are not ways of telling the future or providing mystical experiences. Rather, they are biblical ways of speaking with and encountering God. Prophets, dreamers, and visionaries have a direct link to God's presence and will. For Joel, the presence of these gifts indicates a deep and personal connection to God provided by the Spirit.

The focus of Joel's vision is inclusiveness. *Everyone* receives the Spirit of God. The two references to the Spirit serve as brackets, holding everyone in (vv. 1-2). Sons and daughters, old and young, even male and female slaves will be drenched in God's Spirit. "All flesh" will be inundated with a deeper knowledge of God (v. 1). In its original setting, Joel probably understood "all flesh" as everyone in the Jewish community of Judea. But the ongoing tradition has opened Joel's message to a wider horizon. The apostle Peter refers to this passage in his Pentecost sermon in the book of Acts (2:16-21). For Peter, the outpouring of the Spirit is not only for the Jews from Judea but also Jews from every nation staying in Jerusalem. In Romans 10:12-13, Paul cites Joel 3:5 and extends the gift of the Spirit to "everyone who calls on the name of the Lord." In Paul's understanding, this passage now applies to Gentiles as well as Jews. Joel's vision, which originally asserted inclusiveness within the community of Judah, has been broadened to include literally "all flesh"—everyone.

 The book of Joel is one of the later prophetic books, likely dating around 400 BCE. It is short, consisting of only four chapters. The first two chapters describe a plague of locusts that devastated the harvests of Judah. The book interprets this plague as a prefiguration of the Day of the Lord in which God will judge all the nations. The description of **God's judgment** in chapters 3–4 is vengeful, but it is fundamentally a call for justice. Joel knows that society is not as it should be—children are being sold into slavery for the price of a cup of wine (4:3). God is not indifferent. God promises a better world, the world that Joel sees in the famous vision of Joel 3:1-2 when God pours out the Spirit on all people.

Contemporary Relevance: In Joel 3:1-5, the Spirit affirms the dignity and equality of all people. Joel's vision reveals that God desires a world in which the fundamental value of every person is respected. God is creating a world in which every distinction of age, sex, and social class will be swept away in the outpouring of the Spirit.

Joel calls us to be an inclusive community, insisting that God desires a world in which all have equal access to the goods of creation. All should be able to share in the basics of life: nutrition, shelter, health care, education, employment, and the opportunity for personal development. Whenever we hear that any segment of society is being denied such basic rights, it is our role, as people of faith, to work against such inequities. God's Spirit is poured out on all. All should be able to stand as true participants in the inclusive society God wishes to fashion.

The Spirit Provides Leaders for Justice

Even as Ezekiel and Joel envision the Spirit as the permanent possession of God's people, other scriptural authors present God's Spirit as a gift to future leaders who will guide Israel in God's ways. This lesson will conclude by examining three passages from the book of Isaiah that describe leaders whom the Spirit will inspire to establish God's justice on earth.

The book of Isaiah includes material from several different periods of Israel's history. Chapters 1–39 consist of oracles delivered by Isaiah, the son of Amoz. He served as a prophet to several kings of Israel at the end of the eighth century BCE. These chapters are often called First Isaiah. Chapters 40–55 (often called Second Isaiah) are the words of another prophet, some two hundred years later, who announces Israel's release from captivity in Babylon. Chapters 56–66 (Third Isaiah) are generally thought to include oracles given by a prophet after the return from exile, when Israel was under Persian rule.

The first of our three passages comes from First Isaiah:

Isaiah 11:1-5

The Ideal Davidic King. ¹But a shoot shall sprout from the stump of Jesse,
  and from his roots a bud shall blossom.
²The spirit of the LORD shall rest upon him:
  a spirit of wisdom and of understanding,
A spirit of counsel and of strength,
  a spirit of knowledge and of fear of the LORD,
³and his delight shall be the fear of the LORD.

Not by appearance shall he judge,
  nor by hearsay shall he decide,
⁴But he shall judge the poor with justice,
  and decide fairly for the land's afflicted.
He shall strike the ruthless with the rod of his mouth,
  and with the breath of his lips he shall slay the wicked.
⁵Justice shall be the band around his waist,
  and faithfulness a belt upon his hips.

Isaiah, the son of Amoz, has become disenchanted with the kings of Judah. They are not fulfilling their responsibilities. The royal line of David has become a "stump," a tree that has been cut down (v. 1). From this stump nothing can grow, so Isaiah envisions a new and better ruler, one who will "sprout" from the Davidic line. This ruler will enact all that the previous kings failed to accomplish. Just as the Spirit rushed upon David when Samuel anointed him (1 Sam 16:13), God's Spirit will rest on this new ruler and enable him to execute his office successfully (v. 2).

Israel, and, indeed, the entire Ancient Near East, had a definite expectation of what a good king should do. He was to execute justice. Justice is God's plan for right relations in society. The king will not be obliged to human power and will not be impressed by appearance or swayed by hearsay (v. 3). His responsibility will be to protect the rights of the vulnerable because they are powerless to do so themselves (v. 4). Such care for the poor and marginalized is a central demand of the Jewish tradition. Psalm 72 expresses this belief in the expectations for the king: "O God, give your judgment to the king; / your justice to the king's son; / That he may govern your people with justice, / your oppressed with right judgment, / . . . / That he may defend the oppressed among the people, / save the children of the poor and crush the oppressor" (72:2, 4). The rule of the king is measured by the way justice is extended to the weakest members of the community.

The Spirit of God will equip the future king for his role. He will receive gifts of wisdom, understanding, counsel, strength, knowledge, and fear of the Lord (v. 2). These are qualities the king needs to execute justice. Later tradition has extended these virtues to every Christian. We know them as the "gifts of the Holy Spirit."

The *Catechism of the Catholic Church* enumerates the **seven gifts of the Holy Spirit** as wisdom, understanding, counsel, fortitude, knowledge, piety, and fear of the Lord (1831). The list of these gifts comes from Isaiah 11:1-5, where they are presented as qualities of the Spirit given to the future king. Isaiah, however, names only six qualities. "Piety" does not occur in Isaiah, but because Isaiah mentions "fear of the LORD" twice, early translators used "piety" in place of the first occurrence of "fear of the LORD." This adjustment brought the total number of gifts to seven, which was universally recognized as a perfect number.

Contemporary Relevance: The gifts of the Holy Spirit are familiar to many Catholics. They often serve as a focus for preparation for the sacrament of confirmation. As we reflect on the meaning of these gifts, it is helpful to understand the context in which they were first enumerated. Isaiah presents them as qualities that will allow the king to bring about justice.

In our lives, then, these gifts are intended to equip us to work for justice in our own communities. Wisdom, understanding, strength, and the other gifts are given to us so that we may be empowered to take up the fight against evil. The gifts of the Holy Spirit are not merely virtues to deepen our spiritual lives and bring us closer to God. They are powerful tools with which we are expected to build a new world.

The second passage to be examined comes from Second Isaiah:

Isaiah 42:1-4

The Servant of the Lord. [1]Here is my
 servant whom I uphold,
 my chosen one with whom I am pleased.
Upon him I have put my spirit;
 he shall bring forth justice to the nations.
[2]He will not cry out, nor shout,
 nor make his voice heard in the street.
[3]A bruised reed he will not break,
 and a dimly burning wick he will not
  quench.
He will faithfully bring forth justice.
[4]He will not grow dim or be bruised
 until he establishes justice on the earth;
 the coastlands will wait for his teaching.

The message of these verses was likely delivered to Jews toward the end of the exile in Babylon. Isaiah 42:1-4 is part of the first of four "servant songs" found in the book of Isaiah (42:1-9; 49:1-7; 50:4-11; 52:13–53:12). All four songs refer to someone identified as "God's servant." The word "servant" should not be understood in a diminished sense, as in "slave" or "domestic underling." God's servant is a carefully chosen representative with whom God is "pleased" (42:1). Beginning with Mark's Gospel, which uses this text at Jesus' baptism (1:11), Christians have seen Jesus as this servant. But in its original context, the identity of the servant is ambiguous. Sometimes it seems to refer to an unidentified individual, and other times it appears to refer to Israel as a people.

There is, however, no doubt concerning the mission of the servant. Again, as in the future leader of Isaiah 11:1-5, he is to bring about justice. He is to enact God's plan for the proper ordering of society with special attention to its most vulnerable members. Isaiah 42:1-4 refers to "justice" three times (vv. 1, 3, 4). God has chosen this servant to establish God's justice on earth (v. 4). The action of the servant, however, is not to be like the actions of worldly rulers. He will not be given armies or weapons with which to assert God's rule. He will establish justice through nonviolence. Those who are fragile and damaged ("a bruised reed") will not be sacrificed to reach his goal. Those who are weak and seem expendable ("a dimly burning wick") will not be snuffed out to fulfill his mission (v. 3). God's servant will shun every form of force or coercion. In the eyes of the world, his approach will seem foolish and doomed to fail. God's servant, however, will have a power that upends human strength: God's Spirit (v. 1). Only the Spirit of God can establish God's justice without the use of force.

Contemporary Relevance: Many might see the first servant song as wishful thinking. We are generally opposed to violence, yet we are willing to revise that conviction if the need arises. Babylon, Rome, Russia, and the United States have all used economic and military force to achieve their purposes. Many businesses roll over people and values to protect the bottom line. Some families replace dialogue and consensus with manipulation and shame to instill uniformity.

The first servant song stimulates our imaginations to discover a nonviolent path to God's justice. It challenges every human temptation to believe that force can establish God's kingdom. It questions whether brutal blows can ever engender peace. And it warns that before we commit ourselves to any action of power, we should listen to the promptings of God's Spirit. We know how to use force. It is the role of the Spirit to show us a peaceful way to the justice God desires.

The final passage to be considered is from Third Isaiah. It addresses the circumstances of the Jews after the return from exile:

Isaiah 61:1-4

The Anointed Bearer of Glad Tidings.
  [1]The spirit of the Lord GOD is upon me,
  because the LORD has anointed me;

He has sent me to bring good news to the afflicted,
  to bind up the brokenhearted,
To proclaim liberty to the captives,
  release to the prisoners,
  [2]To announce a year of favor from the LORD
  and a day of vindication by our God;
To comfort all who mourn;
  [3]to place on those who mourn in Zion
  a diadem instead of ashes,
To give them oil of gladness instead of mourning,
  a glorious mantle instead of a faint spirit.
Restoration and Blessing.
They will be called oaks of justice,
  the planting of the LORD to show his glory.
  [4]They shall rebuild the ancient ruins,
  the former wastes they shall raise up
And restore the desolate cities,
  devastations of generation upon generation.

The focus of this passage is on rebuilding (v. 4). The exiles have returned to a devastated Jerusalem. Its ancient edifices, including the temple, were destroyed. But rebuilding is more than bricks and mortar. Society, too, must be rebuilt following the plan of God. The agents of such reconstruction are the people themselves. The blueprint is again the justice of God. The people are called "oaks of justice" (v. 3). They will build the new society in accord with God's will. The prophet who speaks in this passage echoes the servant of Second Isaiah, claiming God's Spirit and the establishment of justice (v. 1). His message emphasizes what is already well known within the Jewish tradition: justice does not begin with the privileged and strong. The first concern of justice is with the afflicted and brokenhearted, with prisoners and those who mourn. God's justice addresses and vindicates those who are forgotten and those who are without power. It is measured by how the least in society are protected and served.

Contemporary Relevance: The saving work of Jesus stands at the center of the gospel and flows easily from the Jewish tradition of which he was a part. We should therefore recognize the strong continuity that exists between the values treasured by Israel and the gospel proclaimed by Jesus. Jesus' mission was one of justice, consciously directed to those who were poor and outcast. His message was not an innovation but rather the lifting up of a central Jewish conviction in which Jesus was nurtured and educated. Jesus proclaimed good news for the marginalized because he was Jewish.

The Gospel writers understood this continuity and characterized Jesus' ministry as good news for the poor. Luke particularly emphasizes this perspective, situating the beginning of Jesus' work in the synagogue of Nazareth (4:16-30). There, Jesus reads Isaiah 61:1-2 as the appropriate description of his mission. The two testaments of the Bible stand in continuity; the Spirit of God unites them to each other.

Israel's dream for a future in which a just society cares for the marginalized burns in the heart of Jesus. It is to an examination of his Spirit-driven mission that we will now turn.

EXPLORING LESSON THREE

1. According to the commentary, what is one way the exile changed Israel's life as a people and its relationship with God? How have you experienced "exile" and "return" in your own life?

_____

_____

_____

_____

_____

2. Why is it fitting that Ezekiel presents the action of God's Spirit in the field of dry bones as an act of creation? The commentary explores how both Ezekiel 37 and Genesis 2 show that God acts in two steps to create rather than one. What does this two-step process suggest to you?

_____

_____

_____

_____

_____

3. Have you ever faced a circumstance as utterly hopeless as bringing dry bones to life? This lesson suggests that even in such a circumstance we may be called to speak a message of hope. Can you offer a personal experience of such a situation?

_____

_____

_____

_____

_____

4. The action of the Spirit in the field of dry bones is meant to assure us that there is no problem so complex or debilitating that God cannot change it. What are one or two of the complex problems we must face in our world today? Do you dare in faith to believe that with God's Spirit they can be resolved? Why or why not?

_____

_____

_____

_____

_____

5. God's gift of a new heart in Ezekiel 36 is meant to give Israel the capacity to do what is right. God re-creates Israel so that Israel can do God's will. Do you ever feel God needs to create a new heart in you? What would that "new heart" be like, and what would it allow you to do?

_____

_____

_____

_____

_____

6. Ezekiel insists that God changes Israel not for Israel's sake but for God's sake. God protects God's own holiness by enabling Israel to do what is right. What sense do you make of this unexpected claim?

_____

_____

_____

_____

_____

7. Joel reveals that God desires a society in which all are included with equal access to God and to the goods of creation. Do you believe that such a community is attainable or merely a noble ideal? How does Joel's call for an inclusive society influence your own life of faith?

_____

_____

_____

_____

_____

8. What are the gifts of the Holy Spirit? Choose one of the gifts of the Holy Spirit that you feel is most necessary in the work for justice. Why did you select this particular one?

_____

_____

_____

_____

_____

9. The first servant song in Isaiah 42:1-4 calls us to participate in God's justice through non-violence. How realistic is such a call to you? What steps can you take in your own life to avoid violence in your family, relationships, and society?

_____

_____

_____

_____

_____

CLOSING PRAYER

Prayer

I will remove the heart of stone from your flesh and give you a heart of flesh. I will put my spirit within you . . . (Ezek 36:26-27)

Lord God, re-create us, your people. Replace our stubbornness with love, our weakness with strength, our sadness with joy, our emptiness with your Spirit. Equip us with the gifts that we need to serve you and one another. Today we pray for those who are in special need of your gifts and presence, especially . . .

LESSON FOUR

The Holy Spirit and Jesus

Begin your personal study and group discussion with a simple and sincere prayer such as:

Prayer

Spirit of God, you breathe life into human beings and into your Word. Fill us with your presence as we spend time with your Word and one another. Re-create us and sustain us day by day.

Read pages 62–73, Lesson Four.

Respond to the questions on pages 74–76, Exploring Lesson Four.

The Closing Prayer on page 76 is for your personal use and may be used at the end of group discussion.

THE HOLY SPIRIT AND JESUS

References to God's Spirit increase dramatically in the writings of the New Testament. Although the New Testament is only about one-third of the length of the Hebrew Scriptures, it contains 379 occurrences of *pneuma*, the Greek equivalent to the Hebrew *ruach*. The Greek term carries the same range of meaning found in the Hebrew. It can mean "wind" (John 3:8; Heb 1:7), refer to human breath (Matt 27:50), and even designate the whole human person (1 Thess 5:23). But in 275 occurrences, *pneuma* refers to God's Spirit.

With such an array of occurrences, this study cannot examine every place the New Testament speaks of God's Spirit, so a selective strategy will be used for the next three lessons to discuss the passages that are most important, most confusing, or most relevant to modern life. This lesson will review material from the four Gospels and will explore how Jesus' life and ministry were imbued with the Spirit of God. The remaining two lessons will explore other New Testament writings as we consider the Spirit's activity in the church and at the end of time.

The Spirit and Those Close to Jesus

Luke emphasizes and explicates the role of God's Spirit more than any other evangelist.

His infancy narrative contains numerous references to God's Spirit, emphasizing how those close to Jesus are guided by the Spirit's power.

After a literary prologue (1:1-4), Luke begins his Gospel by announcing the births of John the Baptist and Jesus. The Spirit plays a major role in these scenes. While serving in the temple, John's father, Zechariah, is told by an angel that he will have a son. The angel describes the child's future: "He will be filled with the holy Spirit even from his mother's womb, and he will turn many of the children of Israel to the Lord their God" (1:15-16). When John is born, Zechariah gives thanks to God in

 A note on the capitalization of "Holy Spirit"

When we speak of the Holy Spirit today, we are referring to the Third Person of the Blessed Trinity. This understanding leads us to capitalize both "Holy" and "Spirit" since we are using the term as a name or title. In many scriptural passages, however, references to the Spirit are less developed. For this reason, the New American Bible Revised Edition (NABRE), which is used throughout this study, does not capitalize "holy" or "spirit" when it occurs in the Hebrew Bible (Old Testament). (See page 13.) In the New

Testament the NABRE capitalizes "Spirit" but not "holy." Here the word "holy" is being used as an adjective to describe God's Spirit, rather than as part of a name or title for God's Spirit.

For clarity and consistency, however, we will capitalize "Holy Spirit" throughout the commentary of this study when used as a designation for God. When the word "spirit" is used in a generic sense to designate *wind*, *breath*, or *spirit* and is not directly associated with the divine, "spirit" will remain lowercase.

a canticle (song) that now bears his name. Luke tells us that his prayer is inspired by the Spirit: "Then Zechariah his father, filled with the holy Spirit, prophesied" (1:67).

Both Luke and Matthew recognize that the birth of Jesus occurred in a unique way through the power of God's Spirit. In Matthew's Gospel, Joseph is concerned when Mary, his betrothed wife, is found to be with child. But the story emphasizes that Mary's pregnancy is "through the holy Spirit" (Matt 1:18, 20). Luke agrees with Matthew concerning the special nature of Jesus' birth. Luke presents his understanding in a scene that is one of the most famous passages of the New Testament:

Luke 1:26-38

Announcement of the Birth of Jesus. [26]In the sixth month, the angel Gabriel was sent from God to a town of Galilee called Nazareth, [27]to a virgin betrothed to a man named Joseph, of the house of David, and the virgin's name was Mary. [28]And coming to her, he said, "Hail, favored one! The Lord is with you." [29]But she was greatly troubled at what was said and pondered what sort of greeting this might be. [30]Then the angel said to her, "Do not be afraid, Mary, for you have found favor with God. [31]Behold, you will conceive in your womb and bear a son, and you shall name him Jesus. [32]He will be great and will be called Son of the Most High, and the Lord God will give him the throne of David his father, [33]and he will rule over the house of Jacob forever, and of his kingdom there will be no end." [34]But Mary said to the angel, "How can this be, since I have no relations with a man?" [35]And the angel said to her in reply, "The holy Spirit will come upon you, and the power of the Most High will overshadow you. Therefore the child to be born will be called holy, the Son of God. [36]And behold, Elizabeth, your relative, has also conceived a son in her old age, and this is the sixth month for her who was called barren; [37]for nothing will be impossible for God." [38]Mary said, "Behold, I am the handmaid of the Lord. May it be done to me according to your word." Then the angel departed from her.

Verse 35 clearly attributes the birth of Jesus to the work of God's Spirit. In light of Mary's objection that she has not had sexual relations with a man, this verse indicates that the conception of Jesus will occur without the involvement of a human father.

Luke fills his annunciation scene with many truths about Jesus. Jesus is son of David and "will be great" (v. 32). He is the unique Son of God because of his birth by the Spirit (v. 35). But Luke also carefully shapes this scene to include a truth about Mary. To understand Luke's approach, it is helpful to be familiar with the set patterns or forms often employed by biblical authors. These patterns are used at key moments in the lives of biblical characters. For example, when a child is to be born, the biblical authors often use a "Birth Announcement Form," consisting of four distinct steps: (1) a heavenly person appears, (2) the birth is announced, (3) the name of the child is given, and (4) something about the future of the child is foretold. Examples of this pattern are found in the announcements of the births of Ishmael and Isaac in the book of Genesis (16:11-12; 17:19).

When God calls someone to a specific task or vocation, another pattern is sometimes employed. The "Call Form" also consists of four steps: (1) the divine call is given, (2) the person who is called expresses doubts or questions about the call, (3) divine assurance is offered, and (4) a sign is provided to support this assurance. Examples of this pattern are found in the calls of Moses (Exod 3:10-12) and Jeremiah (Jer 1:4-10).

In the announcement of Jesus' birth, Luke employs both of these forms. He begins with the expected Birth Announcement Form: (1) the angel Gabriel appears, (2) the birth of a son is announced, (3) the name "Jesus" is given, and (4) Jesus' future is foretold. Luke could have stopped here, and Jesus' birth would have been sufficiently proclaimed. But he continues, employing the biblical Call Form. He uses the entire birth announcement as step 1, making it the content of the call (1:26-33). Mary's question to the angel is step 2. Step 3 is Gabriel's assurance that the Holy Spirit will come upon Mary, and the sign of Elizabeth's pregnancy is step 4.

Two distinct biblical patterns have been united by Luke into one seamless whole.

Jesus' birth has been announced, and it is the first step of Mary's call. What Luke does in this scene is exalt Mary by showing that her role as the mother of Jesus is more than biological. She is not a passive vessel. Rather, the biblical Call Form shows her to be a unique agent of God's will. Not only is her motherhood through the Holy Spirit, but her acceptance of the divine call places her among the great figures of biblical history, comparable to Moses and Jeremiah. Through the creative use of biblical patterns, Luke shows how the wonder of our salvation began with Mary's "yes."

Contemporary Relevance: In a world where women continue to strive for equality, both culturally and economically, Luke's annunciation of Jesus' birth is a valuable passage. The Bible was written in a patriarchal culture. The central characters are in large part men. Many passages relegate women to secondary status. Yet Luke's annunciation scene, foundational to his entire Gospel, provides a forceful counter-cultural voice. In fact, from a Christian viewpoint, one can argue that Mary's call is the most important call in Scripture. In her acceptance, our salvation in Christ was inaugurated.

Mary and Zechariah are not the only characters in Luke's infancy account who are filled with the Holy Spirit. God's Spirit also imbues Mary's cousin Elizabeth. When Mary visits her in the hill country of Judah, Elizabeth welcomes her with a greeting inspired by the Holy Spirit (1:41). Christians have joined Elizabeth's words to those of Gabriel at the annunciation to form our most popular Marian prayer: "Hail, favored one! The Lord is with you" (1:28) and "Most blessed are you among women, and blessed is the fruit of your womb" (1:42). Drawn primarily from Luke's infancy narrative, the Hail Mary has become a daily prayer for millions of believers. It expresses Mary's unique role in our salvation through the Holy Spirit.

 The following charts illustrate the use of the "Birth Announcement Form" and the "Call Form" in Luke 1:26-38. Note that the entire birth announcement serves as the content of Mary's call.

Birth Announcement Form		
A heavenly person appears	The angel Gabriel appears	1:26-29
The birth is announced	The birth of a son is announced to Mary	1:30-31
The name of the child is given	The name "Jesus" is given	1:31
Something about the future of the child is foretold	Jesus' future is foretold	1:32-33

Call Form		
The divine call is given	Jesus' birth announcement serves as Mary's call	1:26-33
The person called expresses doubts or questions	Mary questions the angel	1:34
Divine assurance is offered	Gabriel assures Mary that the Holy Spirit will come upon her	1:35
A sign is provided	Elizabeth's miraculous pregnancy is offered as a sign	1:36-37

Although the first part of the **Hail Mary** comes from the Gospel of Luke, the biblical words were not used as a prayer until the eleventh century CE, when they began to be prayed by monastic orders. The second part of the prayer is a later, non-biblical intercession: "Holy Mary, Mother of God, pray for us sinners, now and at the hour of our death." It was added to the prayer around the time of the Council of Trent (around 1550 CE). Pope Pius V officially included the full form of the prayer in the Roman Breviary in 1568 CE. The Hail Mary is a part of both the Angelus and the Rosary, thus making it a significant part of the prayer life of the church.

One more character is filled with the Spirit in Luke's infancy narrative. When Mary and Joseph present the child Jesus in the temple, they encounter Simeon:

Luke 2:25-32

²⁵Now there was a man in Jerusalem whose name was Simeon. This man was righteous and devout, awaiting the consolation of Israel, and the holy Spirit was upon him. ²⁶It had been revealed to him by the holy Spirit that he should not see death before he had seen the Messiah of the Lord. ²⁷He came in the Spirit into the temple; and when the parents brought in the child Jesus to perform the custom of the law in regard to him, ²⁸he took him into his arms and blessed God, saying:

²⁹"Now, Master, you may let your servant go in peace, according to your word,
³⁰for my eyes have seen your salvation,
³¹which you prepared in sight of all the peoples,
³²a light for revelation to the Gentiles, and glory for your people Israel."

This is the only place Simeon appears in the Bible. He is described as "righteous and devout" (v. 25), characteristics that place him among the other faithful Jews populating Luke's infancy narrative: Zechariah, Elizabeth, Mary, Joseph, and the prophetess Anna (2:36-38). Three times in this brief passage, Simeon is connected to the Spirit: the Spirit is "upon him" (v. 25), the Spirit makes him a promise (v. 26), and the Spirit leads him into the temple to fulfill the promise (v. 27).

The promise to Simeon is profound: before he dies, he will see "the Messiah of the Lord" (v. 26). Luke is well aware of the Spirit-filled leader described in Isaiah 61:2, one who will "comfort all who mourn." Simeon will directly benefit from this promise. He is in need of comfort as he awaits "the consolation of Israel" (v. 25). When Simeon takes the child Jesus in his arms, he holds the comfort promised to all peoples (vv. 31-32).

Contemporary Relevance: Luke does not tell us how old Simeon was when the Holy Spirit promised him that he would live to see God's Messiah. Tradition suggests that he was old and had waited his entire life. The "now" of verse 29 (which is in an emphatic position in the Greek text) supports this interpretation. Now, after a lifetime of waking each day saying, "Maybe today will be the day." Now, after so many occasions of doubt: "Did I hear correctly? Did God really promise me?" Now, at last, Simeon can say, "I behold the Messiah."

All of us wait for good things in our lives. Simeon shows us how to wait with faith and patience. Faith is necessary to believe that the good things God's Spirit promises will come to us. Patience is required so that we can hold on, knowing the Spirit might take time to deliver on those promises. The time frame for the promise made to Simeon was the span of his entire life. In a similar way, we are seldom promised anything by a specific delivery date. The Spirit does not usually say, "You will find someone to love and marry by your next birthday. You will secure a new job by next week. Your granddaughter will stop abusing drugs by summer vacation." When God gives us a promise, we must wait without knowing when it will be fulfilled, believing that we have not been forgotten. We stand, then, with Simeon. In faith, we believe that Christ has come, and his promises to us are real. In patience, we understand that the fulfillment of those promises may not arrive today.

The Spirit and Jesus' Ministry

The Gospels routinely associate God's Spirit with Jesus during his ministry. Before Jesus begins his work, John the Baptist announces that Jesus will baptize with the Holy Spirit (Matt 3:11; Mark 1:8; Luke 3:16). The cry of John the Baptist sets the stage for Jesus' appearance. That expectation is fulfilled when Jesus is baptized by John in the Jordan:

Mark 1:9-11

The Baptism of Jesus. ⁹It happened in those days that Jesus came from Nazareth of Galilee and was baptized in the Jordan by John. ¹⁰On coming up out of the water he saw the heavens being torn open and the Spirit, like a dove, descending upon him. ¹¹And a voice came from the heavens, "You are my beloved Son; with you I am well pleased."

The descent of the Spirit is central to Mark's shaping of this scene. Matthew and Luke follow Mark in their accounts of Jesus' baptism, also attesting to the Spirit's descent (Matt 3:16; Luke 3:22). Although John's Gospel does not describe Jesus' baptism, it, too, recognizes the role of the Spirit: "John [the Baptist] testified further, saying, 'I saw the Spirit come down like a dove from the sky and remain upon him'" (1:32). All four Gospels understand that the ministry of Jesus is inspired and guided by the Spirit of God.

Although Mark's baptism scene only consists of three verses, it is packed with biblical references. Mark is determined to convey that this was no ordinary baptism, nor was Jesus one of John's usual recipients. The tearing open of the heavens (v. 10) indicates a revelation from God (see Isa 63:19; Ezek 1:1), and the words of the "voice [that] came from the heavens" (v. 11) associate Jesus with the Spirit-filled servant of Isaiah 42 who is pleasing to God (see Isa 42:1).

The significance of the Spirit descending upon Jesus "like a dove" is a bit more difficult to interpret (v. 10). The dove is perhaps the best-known symbol of the Holy Spirit, but the only biblical passages that associate the Spirit with a dove are the four Gospel scenes mentioned above. The symbolism of the dove is therefore unclear. Doves seldom appear in the Bible. When they do, a connection to the Holy Spirit is not obvious. Noah releases a dove from the ark (Gen 8:8). The beloved in the Song of Songs is called a dove (2:14). Jesus teaches that we should be as innocent as doves (Matt 10:16). Do these passages indicate that the Spirit descending on Jesus should be understood as free, beloved, or innocent? Possibly. Yet no consistent meaning connects the Spirit and the dove. Perhaps the image of the dove is meant to be as elusive as the Spirit it represents.

One more possible meaning of the dove is worth considering. The Jewish Talmud associates the dove with God's voice: "I heard a divine voice cooing like a dove" (Berachot 3a). Understanding the dove in this way inserts a gentle dimension into the scene of Jesus' baptism. In the midst of a passage in which the heavens are torn open with cosmic drama, the descent of the dove may point to Jesus' serene conviction that he is the Son in whom God is pleased. The dove, then, might indicate God's soft murmuring assurance that Jesus is forever loved.

Contemporary Relevance: There are many miracles in our lives that are not dramatic. God's Spirit may descend on us in ways that are both ordinary and gentle. We watch our children play and suddenly realize how blessed we are and how thankful we should be. We witness a friend demonstrate generosity and begin to think that we, too, should be generous to an enemy. We sit in silence watching the snow fall outside our window and suddenly feel a prompt to move our lives in a new direction. God can certainly shake and shock us, pulling us up by the nape of our necks. But God also works in subtle, quiet ways. That is why we must be attentive. We do not want to miss the gentle breeze of God's Spirit. We need to hear the soft cooing of God's voice.

The Talmud refers to the oral traditions by which the Jewish community interprets Tanak (the law, prophets, and writings that Christians refer to as the Old Testament). The Talmud consists of two parts: the Mishnah (written at the end of the second century CE) and the Gemara (written in the fourth–sixth centuries CE). Although these written forms of the Talmud are dated much later than the Christian Gospels, some of the sayings and traditions within them may date to the time of Jesus.

We have already seen how, at his baptism, Mark associates Jesus with the Spirit-filled servant of Isaiah 42. Matthew makes this connection even more explicit. After a reference to Jesus curing the sick, Matthew connects Jesus' action of mercy with God's servant by quoting Isaiah 42:

Matthew 12:15-21

The Chosen Servant. ¹⁵When Jesus realized this, he withdrew from that place. Many [people] followed him, and he cured them all, ¹⁶but he warned them not to make him known. ¹⁷This was to fulfill what had been spoken through Isaiah the prophet:
¹⁸"Behold, my servant whom I have chosen,
    my beloved in whom I delight;
I shall place my spirit upon him,
    and he will proclaim justice to the Gentiles.
¹⁹He will not contend or cry out,
    nor will anyone hear his voice in the streets.

---

²⁰A bruised reed he will not break,
    a smoldering wick he will not quench,
    until he brings justice to victory.
²¹And in his name the Gentiles will hope."

Matthew quotes passages from the Hebrew Scriptures more frequently than any other evangelist. This is his longest citation, clearly indicating its importance to his understanding of Jesus' ministry. Although Matthew's citation does not follow the Hebrew text exactly (nor even the later Greek translations of the Hebrew), he is clearly referencing Isaiah 42:1-4. Jesus is again presented as God's servant in whom God delights. The use of this reference in Matthew's Gospel is clear: God's Spirit allows Jesus to enact God's justice (vv. 18, 20).

Luke is even more forceful in connecting Jesus with the Spirit. He informs us that Jesus was "[f]illed with the holy Spirit" and "led by the Spirit into the desert" (4:1; see also Matt 4:1; Mark 1:12). He then dramatically highlights the Spirit in a scene in Jesus' hometown of Nazareth:

Jesus teaching

> ### Luke 4:16-21
>
> **The Rejection at Nazareth.** [16]He came to Nazareth, where he had grown up, and went according to his custom into the synagogue on the sabbath day. He stood up to read [17]and was handed a scroll of the prophet Isaiah. He unrolled the scroll and found the passage where it was written:
> [18]"The Spirit of the Lord is upon me,
>   because he has anointed me
>   to bring glad tidings to the poor.
> He has sent me to proclaim liberty to captives
>   and recovery of sight to the blind,
>   to let the oppressed go free,
> [19]and to proclaim a year acceptable to the Lord."
> [20]Rolling up the scroll, he handed it back to the attendant and sat down, and the eyes of all in the synagogue looked intently at him. [21]He said to them, "Today this scripture passage is fulfilled in your hearing."

Unlike Mark, Luke places this scene at Nazareth at the very beginning of Jesus' public ministry, presenting it as an overture to his entire Gospel. A passage from Isaiah 61:1-2 provides the primary focus. Jesus is the anointed, Spirit-filled leader whom God has promised (v. 18). His mission is to bring glad tidings to the poor, captives, blind, and oppressed. We have already seen how the Hebrew Bible associates God's justice with the poor and marginalized (Lesson Three). More than any other Gospel writer, Luke connects this theme to Jesus' ministry (v. 21). Throughout Luke's Gospel, Jesus is concerned with the economically and socially poor. His mission is to proclaim God's care for the weak and to announce a new world order in which the vulnerable will no longer be afflicted or forgotten.

Contemporary Relevance: In Luke's Gospel, Jesus calls us to reach out beyond our concern for ourselves and those close to us. He announces that God's desire is to clean up the messes of our world, where so many are left behind. To be disciples of Jesus, we must do more than protect the good that is ours. Avoiding sin, saying prayers, and going to church are not enough. The Spirit calls followers of Jesus to take up God's work of changing this hurting world. The mission is not only to feed the poor but to undo structures that perpetuate poverty and lessen human dignity. The challenge is not only to free those unjustly imprisoned or bought and sold in modern forms of slavery but to attack the societal and economic forces that allow and foster injustice and human enslavement. Adopting the words of Isaiah 61:1-2, Jesus calls us to roll up our sleeves, cooperate with the Spirit, and build the kingdom of God.

 Scholars are confident that Luke used two main sources in the composition of his Gospel. the Gospel of Mark and a collection of Jesus' sayings, often identified as "Q." The sequence of Luke's Gospel basically follows Mark's outline. The scene at Nazareth (Luke 4:14-21), however, is a clear departure from this practice. In Mark's Gospel, Jesus does not minister in Nazareth until the end of his work in Galilee (Mark 6:1-6a). Luke moves this scene to the beginning of Jesus' ministry. Although he retains some of Mark's material, he adds his own, including the quotation from Isaiah 61:1-2. In this way, **Luke shapes this scene** to highlight the themes that are important to him and his community.

So far, we have reviewed the activity of the Spirit at the beginning of Jesus' ministry. The Spirit is also present as Jesus carries out his mission. This is shown in a particular way through Jesus' miracles. The most frequent type of miracle in the Gospels is the expulsion of demons. Such miracles demonstrate Jesus' power over evil and anticipate the establishment of God's kingdom through Jesus' death and resurrection. In a debate with his opponents, Jesus reveals the purpose of these mighty works and the role of the Holy Spirit in their completion: "But if it is by the Spirit of God that I drive out demons, then the kingdom of God has come upon you" (Matt 12:28). This is the purpose of all the miracles of Jesus. He does not cure a blind person or heal someone who is paralyzed simply for the sake of that individual. His miracles are also signs that the Spirit is active, empowering Jesus to bring about God's reign.

Jesus' preaching ministry also conveys several important ideas about the Holy Spirit. One particular teaching has puzzled Christians since the time of the early church. All three Synoptic Gospels include this enigmatic teaching of Jesus about the Holy Spirit: "Amen, I say to you, all sins and all blasphemies that people utter will be forgiven them. But whoever blasphemes against the holy Spirit will never have forgiveness, but is guilty of an everlasting sin" (Mark 3:28-29; see also Matt 12:31-32; Luke 12:10). In this saying, Jesus seems to be speaking about a particular sin that is so heinous that it can never be forgiven. However, the context of the saying reveals a deeper issue. In this passage, Jesus' entire ministry is being challenged. Some in the crowd are claiming that his work is not of God but of Satan (Mark 3:22). What is at stake, therefore, is not a particular personal sin but the wholesale rejection of God's Spirit in Jesus' teaching and deeds. This rejection is not the result of honest doubt. It is made by those who know full well the validity of Jesus' mission but purposefully close their hearts to it. Such blasphemy cannot be forgiven. This is not because God is unwilling to forgive but because those who blaspheme are not open to the forgiveness that is offered.

Contemporary Relevance: Jesus' teaching about the Holy Spirit in Mark 3:28-29 communicates the seriousness with which God regards human freedom. God is at work in our world to save it. God makes every effort to offer us love and grace. But God will never force anyone to accept such gifts. Every person remains free to recognize and accept God's blessings, or to deny and reject them—not out of doubt but out of willfulness. As foolish and as destructive as such a choice would be, God's love, like human love, can be refused. Doing so is to blaspheme against the Holy Spirit. It is a denial of the goodness and presence of God.

Another saying from Jesus' ministry begins with a description of Jesus' own experience of the Spirit. Luke writes, "At that very moment he rejoiced [in] the holy Spirit and said, 'I give you praise, Father, Lord of heaven and earth, for although you have hidden these things from the wise and the learned you have revealed them to the childlike. Yes, Father, such has been your gracious will'" (10:21). Jesus is always guided by the Spirit, but in this passage the Spirit leads him to a dramatic insight: the depths of the gospel are most clearly understood by the poor and lowly. A child with no status or power is uniquely capable of embracing God's love. This truth, so contrary to human expectations, fills Jesus with joy.

Luke 10:21 is an example of a theme within Luke's Gospel that is often called "the great reversal." It asserts that God values people and human actions in a way that reverses our expectations. Instead of extolling the rich and powerful, God cares for the marginalized and forgotten. Early in Luke's Gospel, Mary's *Magnificat* praises God as the one who throws down rulers from their thrones and lifts up the lowly (1:52). The theme repeats in the parable of the Prodigal Son, where the unworthy son, not the faithful one, is welcomed by his father's embrace (15:11-32); in the story of the poor beggar Lazarus, who is raised up to glory in the bosom of Abraham, whereas the rich man is not (16:19-31); and in the account of Jesus choosing to stay at the house of Zacchaeus, a despised tax collector, rather than in the home of a more acceptable candidate (19:1-10). The joy of Jesus in Luke 10:21 adds its own voice to the great reversal of Luke's Gospel. It is not the wise who understand what is truly important but children. Such insight is a gift of the Holy Spirit.

Contemporary Relevance: What matters most in life is not the complex computations of advanced minds nor the impressive accomplishments of those in power. In fact, those who live entirely on that sophisticated level may never appreciate life's deepest treasures. Children, however, can perceive what is essential to life: fairness, compassion, and the power of love.

Seeing with the eyes of a child becomes possible when other desires do not clutter our lives. The drive to accumulate more prestige, more influence, more possessions does not enhance our existence but complicates it. Bigger egos, larger homes, and deeper bank accounts will not necessarily free us. They can enslave us. We find ourselves managing what we own rather than living who we are. We have more options but less life, more possessions but less joy. The Spirit of God reveals the illusion of such shallow promises and focuses our souls on the gifts of faith, hope, and love. The Spirit gives us the freedom to let go of what will never satisfy us and to hold tight to the values that bring us joy. God's Spirit knows that it is a gift to be simple and allows us to embrace our lives as children of God.

The Gospels not only show the Spirit working in Jesus but also promise that the Spirit will be given to those who belong to Jesus. Luke 11:9-13 speaks of receiving the Holy Spirit in prayer:

Luke 11:9-13

The Answer to Prayer. [9]"And I tell you, ask and you will receive; seek and you will find; knock and the door will be opened to you. [10]For everyone who asks, receives; and the one who seeks, finds; and to the one who knocks, the door will be opened. [11]What father among you would hand his son a snake when he asks for a fish? [12]Or hand him a scorpion when he asks for an egg? [13]If you then, who are wicked, know how to give good gifts to your children, how much more will the Father in heaven give the holy Spirit to those who ask him?"

In this passage, Jesus offers a comparison between human and divine love to illustrate his teaching on prayer. His strategy is to use examples of human goodness and then assert "how much more" goodness belongs to God. His characterization of humans as "wicked" must be understood in this context (v. 13). The intention is not to color us as morally depraved but only to reveal how far even our good actions fall short when compared to those of God.

Contemporary Relevance: Although these words concerning prayer are comforting, they pose a problem. From experience we realize that many of the things for which we pray are not granted. How can we square Jesus' promises with the reality of unanswered prayers? This passage reminds us that *what we pray for* is not really at the heart of prayer. The foundation and core of prayer is a *relationship with God* in which we can trust. Jesus' words emphasize such trust. We might ask for a fish—and we may not receive a fish, but we will not be given a snake. We might want an egg—and we may not receive an egg, but we will not find ourselves holding a scorpion.

Jesus is telling us that if we ask for something good, we will receive something good. It might not, however, be the particular good thing we requested. Prayer, then, is an expression of faith, a request for God to act on our behalf. Even if what we request is not granted, we have asked, and God will not ignore us. In fact, what we will always receive is God's own Spirit (v. 13).

The Spirit in the Gospel of John

Like the other three Gospels, John's Gospel clearly associates the Spirit with those who follow Christ. Only through the Spirit can a person profess faith in Jesus and live in union with him. Jesus tells Nicodemus, "Amen, amen, I say to you, no one can enter the kingdom of God without being born of water and Spirit" (John 3:5). Jesus informs the Samaritan woman that proper worship of God must occur in the Spirit: "But the hour is coming, and is now here, when true worshipers will worship the Father in Spirit and truth; and indeed the Father seeks such people to worship him. God is Spirit, and those who worship him must worship in Spirit and truth" (4:23-24). God, through Jesus, gives the Spirit abundantly to those who believe (3:34). It is the Spirit who gives life (6:63).

John's Gospel includes a lengthy farewell address given by Jesus to his disciples before his death. In five places in this farewell address, Jesus speaks of someone he calls "the Paraclete" (14:15-17, 26; 15:26-27; 16:7-14). Jesus says that the Paraclete is sent by the Father (14:26) and will only come when Jesus departs (15:26). The Paraclete is the "Spirit of truth" (14:17; 16:13). This special name or term for the Holy Spirit expresses how the Spirit will be the personal presence of Jesus among believers while Jesus is with the Father. The Greek word *parakletos* has a variety of meanings that give us insight into the Spirit's dynamic presence. The word can mean "witness," "spokesperson," "consoler," "teacher," "defense lawyer," or "helper" (the NABRE translates *parakletos* as "Advocate"). The Holy Spirit assumes all of these functions. The Paraclete does all that Jesus would do for us if he were still bodily with us.

The Holy Spirit assumes special prominence in John's Gospel when Jesus appears after the resurrection. In a locked room, Jesus bestows the Holy Spirit on his disciples:

John 20:19-23

Apperance to the Disciples. ¹⁹On the evening of that first day of the week, when the doors were locked, where the disciples were, for fear of the Jews, Jesus came and stood in their midst and said to them, "Peace be with you." ²⁰When he had said this, he showed them his hands and his side. The disciples rejoiced when they saw the Lord. ²¹[Jesus] said to them again, "Peace be with you. As the Father has sent me, so I send you." ²²And when he had said this, he breathed on them and said to them, "Receive the holy Spirit. ²³Whose sins you forgive are forgiven them, and whose sins you retain are retained."

In John's Gospel the term that is often translated **"the Jews"** is used in a technical sense. Although it can refer to the Jewish people as a whole, it most frequently indicates individuals in the Gospel who are opposed to Jesus. Therefore, because many Jews believed in Jesus, there are Jews who are not part of "the Jews." This is obvious in John 20:19-20. If the doors were locked to keep out "the Jews" (v. 19), who was being locked in? All of the disciples were Jewish. Because the Gospel of John clearly associates "the Jews" with Jesus' death, it is important to recognize that not all Jews are included in that designation. Overlooking this point could support the false claim that the Jewish people were responsible for the death of Jesus.

Although Luke presents the Spirit descending upon the early church on the feast of Pentecost (Acts 2:1-41), in John's Gospel the Spirit is given on the night of the resurrection. The gift of the Spirit marks a new phase of salvation: the work of Jesus now continues under the guidance of the Spirit. The solemnity of this moment is recognized by John. When Jesus gives the Spirit to the disciples, he "breathe[s]" on them (v. 22), a clear mirroring of God's act of creating in Genesis (2:7). Just as the breath of God gave life to the first human, the gift of the Spirit gives life to the disciples to carry out Jesus' mission. The community of Jesus' followers is the instrument of a new creation.

This resurrection narrative also closely links the giving of the Spirit with the theme of forgiveness. Not only does Jesus commission the disciples to forgive the sins of others (v. 23), but his double greeting of peace indicates that he forgives his disciples after their failure to stand with him in his passion and death (vv. 19, 21). Yet this passage also suggests that the *consequences* of sin cannot be completely wiped away. Even though Jesus is glorified, wounds remain on his risen body. The sin of Jesus' death at the hands of the Romans, the failure of Peter's denial, the fault of the disciples' absence during Jesus' suffering are incised into his hands and side. When Jesus shows his disciples the marks of his passion, he is reminding them that although his suffering is past and they are forgiven, the aftereffects of violence and betrayal remain. It is not possible to return to the way things were before his death. Sin and failure leave marks that cannot be erased.

Contemporary Relevance: When we fail in some significant way, there is always the possibility of forgiveness. But we must also have the strength to face the consequences of what we have done. If out of selfishness or fear we betray a friend, we can be reconciled. But we will always know that we placed something unworthy above the value of that relationship. If we break a confidence or tell a lie that seriously hurts someone, we can repent. But even if we are forgiven, we will always remember that we were weak enough to hurt another person. The wounds of our sins can be healed, but the marks of those wounds remain with us in some way. Years later, when we remember our failure, we may find ourselves wondering, *Was I really that selfish? Was I actually that weak? Did I fall so short from the person I was called to be?*

John 20:19-23 cautions us not to be naive. Our failures, though forgiven, have ongoing effects. And yet this passage offers us hope. The wounds of Jesus are displayed on a glorified body. The disciples are flawed, but they receive Jesus' peace and forgiveness. Even though the consequences of sin cannot be completely erased, with God's help we find the strength to live with what we cannot change. God's Spirit gives us the courage to accept the marks of our healed wounds and continue in God's service.

The Great Commission

The last passage to be examined in this lesson is found at the conclusion of Matthew's Gospel:

Matthew 28:16-20

The Commissioning of the Disciples. [16]The eleven disciples went to Galilee, to the mountain to which Jesus had ordered them. [17]When they saw him, they worshiped, but they doubted. [18]Then Jesus approached and said to them, "All power in heaven and on earth has been given to me. [19]Go, therefore, and make disciples of all nations, baptizing them in the name of the Father, and of the Son, and of the holy Spirit, [20]teaching them to observe all that I have commanded you. And behold, I am with you always, until the end of the age."

Often called "The Great Commission," this passage emphasizes that the triumph initiated by Jesus' resurrection is not complete until the kingdom of God is established in its fullness (v. 20). Disciples of Jesus are to build that kingdom by spreading his teachings and baptizing in the name of the Father, Son, and Holy Spirit (v. 19). This is the only place in the New Testament where the "Spirit" is mentioned with the "Father" and "Son" in the formulation that has become so familiar to us as the sign of the cross. The wording probably derives from an early Christian baptismal formula. Matthew's words are not a profession of the Trinity. Such a defined affirmation will only come with time, as the church grows in its understanding of God's revelation. But Matthew's words provide a biblical starting point from which the later doctrine of the Trinity develops. Matthew's purpose here is not to reveal the inner life of God but to assure his readers that the Spirit is an essential force in the work of every disciple.

Those who are commissioned are far from perfect. The ominous mention of the "eleven" (v. 16) is a reminder that Jesus was betrayed by one of the twelve. When the risen Christ appears, they worship him, but they also doubt (v. 17). Yet Jesus commissions them all and sends them forth with the Holy Spirit. Matthew thereby promises that the Spirit will compensate for the weakness of the disciples. Jesus might have preferred courageous followers who would stand by him in trials and believe without hesitation. But he is willing to send the disciples as he finds them, relying on the Spirit to accompany and guide them.

Contemporary Relevance: What is true for the disciples is true for us. We are not perfect people, but our flaws do not excuse us from doing what Jesus asks of us. We must love our families even if sometimes we do not love them sufficiently and even if the love we offer is not reciprocated. We must guide our children even when our patience runs thin and the advice we offer is rejected. We must proclaim the good news of the gospel to the world even if our message is quickly dismissed. We will always be able to find others who are more qualified, more motivated, and more holy than we are. But such comparisons are not to the point. Jesus knows all our flaws and sends us anyway. He knows that the Spirit is able to make up the difference between our weakness and the great mission to which we are called.

EXPLORING LESSON FOUR

1. What literary patterns does Luke employ in the annunciation scene in Luke 1:26-38? What does the resulting scene tell us about Mary's role in God's plan?

_____

_____

_____

_____

_____

2. What was the promise the Holy Spirit gave to Simeon (Luke 2:26)? How would you imagine a promise the Holy Spirit might make to you?

_____

_____

_____

_____

_____

3. Which of the many allusions and images that Mark includes in the brief scene of Jesus' baptism in 1:9-11 is most effective in helping you appreciate and understand the role of the Spirit? How does this particular idea or image speak to you?

_____

_____

_____

_____

4. In what sense does Jesus' visit to Nazareth in Luke 4:16-21 serve as the "overture" to Luke's Gospel? What does Luke tell us in this scene about Jesus' role and ministry?

_____

_____

_____

_____

_____

5. According to the commentary, what is the "everlasting sin" that Jesus says can never be forgiven (Mark 3:28-29)? What does this perplexing passage say to you about your relationship with God?

_____

_____

_____

_____

_____

_____

6. Luke 11:9-13 assures us that when we ask for something from God, we will receive the Holy Spirit. What does this mean to you, and how might this perspective enrich or change your prayer life?

_____

_____

_____

_____

_____

_____

7. Who is the Paraclete in John's Gospel, and what does the Paraclete do? Why does Jesus promise a Paraclete to his disciples?

_____

_____

_____

_____

8. a) When is the gift of the Holy Spirit given to the disciples in John's Gospel (John 20:19-23)? Why is the gift appropriately connected to forgiveness?

_____

_____

_____

_____

_____

b) How do you understand the difference between sin, which can be forgiven, and the *consequences* of sin, that can remain with us? Reflect on an occasion when you felt that your sins were forgiven, but you still experienced consequences of sin. What insights can you share, or what questions do you have, based on your experience or the commentary's exploration of this topic?

_____

_____

_____

_____

9. What is Matthew suggesting by ending his Gospel with the Great Commission (28:16-20)? How do the flaws mentioned in the disciples impact their mission? How does this passage speak to your own role as a disciple?

_____

_____

_____

_____

_____

CLOSING PRAYER

Prayer

And when he had said this, he breathed on them and said to them, "Receive the holy Spirit." (John 20:22)

Risen Lord, breathe your Spirit into us, that we may be animated by your vibrant presence. Breathe into us your Spirit of love, your Spirit of peace, your Spirit of healing, and your Spirit of reconciliation. Prepare us to be your faithful disciples, to serve those who are vulnerable, to love one another, and to witness to your saving presence in our world. Today we pray especially for the strength and compassion to serve you by . . .

LESSON FIVE

The Holy Spirit and the Church

Begin your personal study and group discussion with a simple and sincere prayer such as:

Prayer

Spirit of God, you breathe life into human beings and into your Word. Fill us with your presence as we spend time with your Word and one another. Re-create us and sustain us day by day.

Read pages 78–89, Lesson Five.

Respond to the questions on pages 90–92, Exploring Lesson Five.

The Closing Prayer on page 92 is for your personal use and may be used at the end of group discussion.

THE HOLY SPIRIT AND THE CHURCH

Luke is the only Gospel writer who has given us a second volume: the Acts of the Apostles. He has thereby created a narrative that does not end with the death and resurrection of Jesus but continues to describe the activity of the early church.

The Acts of the Apostles could be called the "Book of the Holy Spirit." The Spirit is mentioned more times in Acts than in any other book of the Bible (fifty-five times) and functions as a major character within the narrative, impelling and guiding the plot. Luke's second volume presents the Holy Spirit as the interior dynamic force of the church. Although the relationship between the Holy Spirit and the church is treated in many New Testament texts (some of which we will explore in Lesson Six), we will limit our discussion in this lesson to the Acts of the Apostles, which not only directly addresses the life and growth of the church but also displays Luke's exceptional ability to tell a story.

 Although Luke's second volume is called the **"Acts of the Apostles,"** the name is misleading. Only two apostles are treated in any depth: Peter and Paul. John travels with Peter but has no "acts" of his own. Philip is provided with a few scenes in chapter 8, and the death of James, son of Zebedee, is mentioned (12:2). Moreover, Paul, whose ministry is narrated more than any other character, was not one of the original twelve apostles selected by Jesus. But it was not Luke's intention to enumerate the acts of each of the twelve apostles. He wanted to present the growth of the church through the power of the Holy Spirit.

Luke begins Acts with a prologue addressed to Theophilus ("friend of God" or "beloved of God"), who may have been a patron who supported Luke during his writing. These opening verses reveal what Luke hopes to achieve in his second narrative:

Acts 1:1-9

The Promise of the Spirit. [1]In the first book, Theophilus, I dealt with all that Jesus did and taught [2]until the day he was taken up, after giving instructions through the holy Spirit to the apostles whom he had chosen. [3]He presented himself alive to them by many proofs after he had suffered, appearing to them during forty days and speaking about the kingdom of God. [4]While meeting with them, he enjoined them not to depart from Jerusalem, but to wait for "the promise of the Father about which you have heard me speak; [5]for John baptized with water, but in a few days you will be baptized with the holy Spirit."

The Ascension of Jesus. [6]When they had gathered together they asked him, "Lord, are you at this time going to restore the kingdom to Israel?" [7]He answered them, "It is not for you to know the times or seasons that the Father has established by his own authority. [8]But you will receive power when the holy Spirit comes upon you, and you will be my witnesses in Jerusalem, throughout Judea and Samaria, and to the ends of the earth." [9]When he had said this, as they were looking on, he was lifted up, and a cloud took him from their sight.

The Holy Spirit is mentioned four times in these opening nine verses. Through the Spirit, Jesus gives instruction to the apostles (v. 2). The Spirit is "the promise of the Father" (v. 4) who will be given to the apostles and with whom they will be baptized (v. 5). Most importantly, the Spirit is the power that will allow the apostles to witness to the gospel, the good news of Jesus Christ. Their task is to proclaim the good news "in Jerusalem, throughout Judea and Samaria, and to the ends of the earth" (v. 8). This verse provides the trajectory of the entire book of Acts. As the apostles spread the gospel from Jerusalem to "the ends of the earth" (understood to be Rome), it is the Spirit who time and again moves the story forward and enables the early church to accomplish its mission. Part of Luke's genius is to have constructed his narrative in such a way that we are convinced that nothing can stop the spread of the gospel. The church's mission will not fail, because God's Spirit directs it.

The Spirit Is Poured Out

Certainly, the most famous passage in Acts is the coming of the Spirit upon the apostles at Pentecost:

Acts 2:1-13

The Coming of the Spirit. ¹When the time for Pentecost was fulfilled, they were all in one place together. ²And suddenly there came from the sky a noise like a strong driving wind, and it filled the entire house in which they were. ³Then there appeared to them tongues as of fire, which parted and came to rest on each one of them. ⁴And they were all filled with the holy Spirit and began to speak in different tongues, as the Spirit enabled them to proclaim.

⁵Now there were devout Jews from every nation under heaven staying in Jerusalem. ⁶At this sound, they gathered in a large crowd, but they were confused because each one heard them speaking in his own language. ⁷They were astounded, and in amazement they asked, "Are not all these people who are speaking Galileans? ⁸Then how does each of us hear them in his own native language? ⁹We are Parthians, Medes, and Elamites, inhabitants of Mesopotamia, Judea and Cappadocia, Pontus and Asia, ¹⁰Phrygia and Pamphylia, Egypt and the districts of Libya near Cyrene, as well as travelers from Rome, ¹¹both Jews and converts to Judaism, Cretans and Arabs, yet we hear them speaking in our own tongues of the mighty acts of God." ¹²They were all astounded and bewildered, and said to one another, "What does this mean?" ¹³But others said, scoffing, "They have had too much new wine."

This passage has made an indelible impression upon the Christian imagination, so it may surprise us to notice how brief and elusive it is. Only the first four verses describe the descent of the Spirit. The rest of the passage reports the reaction of the Jewish crowd that has gathered around the apostles. The description of the Spirit is vague and mysterious. A close reading of the text reveals how tentative Luke's imagery is. Luke does not say the house was filled with a strong driving wind but with "a noise *like* a strong driving wind" (v. 2; emphasis added). Fire is often used in the Bible when God appears. Examples include Moses and the burning bush (Exod 3:2), God on Mount Sinai (Deut 4:12), and God's voice (Ps 29:7). Yet Luke reduces the impact of the fire image. He does not say that tongues of fire came upon the disciples. Rather what descended were "tongues *as of* fire" (v. 3; emphasis added). Luke consciously softens the drama of this scene to serve his theological purpose. He does not want us to be distracted by sound, wind, and flame. The real miracle of Pentecost is found in the transformation of the apostles. They are now ready to begin their mission. Empowered by the Spirit, they have been transformed and can now proclaim the mighty works of God (vv. 4, 11).

Yet even with the Spirit's power, God's mission can never be imposed upon anyone. Those who hear the apostles must choose to believe.

This is why Luke ends the scene with a humorous comment. Every person must decide whether what they see and hear before them comes from God's Spirit or "too much new wine" (v. 13).

Pentecost means "fifty." It refers to the Jewish feast of Weeks, which is established in Leviticus 23:15-22 to take place fifty days after the feast of Unleavened Bread. At Pentecost, thanksgiving was offered for the firstfruits of the wheat harvest. This feast provides a fitting context for Luke's descent of the Spirit in Acts 2:1-13, for the subsequent mission of the apostles is the firstfruits of the gospel that will lead to the full harvest at Jesus' return.

Contemporary Relevance: We associate the Holy Spirit with fire because of this passage from Acts 2. Here are two ways to consider how the image of fire speaks to the Spirit's presence.

1) *The Spirit as my fire.* Luke tells us that the tongues as of fire came to rest upon "each one" of the gathered apostles (v. 3). This indicates that the gift of the Spirit comes to us as individuals. The personal gift of the Spirit does not negate the communal nature of the church, but it insists that being church is not like making sausage, where all our particular talents and skills are ground together into an indistinguishable mix. The unique gifts of each individual are essential in spreading God's reign.

Our gifts are not the same. Some are dramatic and others unassuming. Some may be tied to intellectual prowess and others to matters of the heart. Some—like teaching, preaching, and athletic abilities—can be immediately seen. Others are more hidden, such as the gift of recognizing another's pain or the patience to listen when a hurting friend needs to vent. The church is impoverished whenever we fail to use the gifts we have been given. At Pentecost, each disciple was marked with his or her individual flame. If the gospel is to spread to the ends of the earth, we must each find our particular fire and use it.

2) *Fire as warmth, light, and burning.* The richness of a symbol is that it evokes more than one meaning. The image of fire, then, suggests that the Spirit acts in our lives in at least three distinct ways.

We may find ourselves in a cold and empty place. The death of someone we love or a broken relationship has chilled us to the bone. We walk around hollow and numb. Then our five-year-old climbs on our lap and gives us a hug. A friend makes us laugh. Our spouse speaks just the right words of comfort. And for the first time in weeks, we can take a deep breath and feel the blood move again within us. Those moments of humanity and hope that come to us in the cold are the *warmth* of the Holy Spirit's fire.

Sometimes things are confusing and dark. We have problems that we cannot resolve. We don't know how to face a personal financial crisis, how to speak to a teenage son or daughter, how to care for an aging parent. In such confusion, we can become paralyzed. Then we see a small step we can take, a conversation we can begin. That insight, that path through the darkness, is the *light* of the Holy Spirit's fire.

Some things are wrong in our family, in our church, or in our world. Our actions may be facilitating drug or alcohol abuse in our family. We are scandalized by the mishandling of child sexual abuse in our church. We discover that too many politicians are motivated by self-promotion instead of service. We decide that things need to change, and we need to act. That powerful force within us, moving us to do what is right, is the *burning* of the Holy Spirit's fire.

The Holy Spirit comes to us as fire to warm us, enlighten us, and if necessary, even singe us, so that we might know that God is always with us, leading us forward and prompting us to share our own fire at the service of the world around us.

After the descent of the Holy Spirit is described in 2:1-13, Acts continues with a lengthy speech by Peter (2:14-41). In Lesson Three, we read about how the prophet Joel spoke of an outpouring of God's Spirit that would fill up the entire people (Joel 3:1-5). In this speech, Peter uses Joel's prophecy to announce that God's Spirit has now been poured out on the community of Jesus' disciples. This outpouring was made possible by the resurrection of Jesus: "God raised this Jesus; of this we are all witnesses. Exalted at the right hand of God, he received the promise of the holy Spirit from the Father and poured it forth, as you [both] see and hear" (2:32-33). Peter tells the astonished crowd that what they have seen and heard is a Spirit-filled community of witnesses ready to spread the good news.

The Pentecost scene takes place in Jerusalem and marks the beginning of the church's mission. According to Acts, three thousand Jews from many nations were baptized and received the Holy Spirit that day (2:38-41). Pentecost, however, is not the only time the Spirit descends upon believers in Acts. On four other occasions, the Spirit comes upon those who believe. These subsequent descents of the Spirit mark the progress of the apostles' mission as it moves to "the ends of the earth" (1:8). In Acts 4:31, the community in Jerusalem is gathered for prayer when suddenly "the place where they were gathered shook, and they were all filled with the holy Spirit and continued to speak the word of God with boldness." In Acts 8:17, the Spirit comes upon believers in Samaria when Peter and John "la[y] hands on them." In Acts 10:44, the Spirit falls upon the Gentile Cornelius and his household in Caesarea. Finally, the Spirit descends on twelve believers in Ephesus (19:6).

The Spirit permeates the life of the early church, inspiring the preaching of Peter (4:8) and Stephen (7:55), setting Paul and Barnabas apart for mission work (13:2), guiding the selection of assistants to the apostles (6:3), directing the ministry of Philip (8:29, 39), healing Paul of his blindness (9:17-19), inspiring the prophet Agabus (11:28; 21:11), initiating the mission to the Gentiles (10:44-48), directing the council in Jerusalem (15:28), calling Paul to establish communities in Europe (16:6-10), and filling the apostles with joy (13:52). The Spirit dwells within the community, increasing its numbers: "The church throughout all Judea, Galilee, and Samaria was at peace. It was being built up and walked in the fear of the Lord, and with the consolation of the holy Spirit it grew in numbers" (9:31).

Always and in every place, the fundamental purpose of the Spirit is to enable witness to Jesus so that the gospel might spread. As Peter says in the trial before the Sanhedrin, "We are witnesses of these things, as is the holy Spirit that God has given to those who obey him" (5:32).

The Spirit Protects the Church

The spread of the gospel takes place in a world where evil forces oppose God's will. Although the Spirit guarantees that the mission will be successful, Luke includes stories in which individuals attempt to frustrate the plan of God. The role of the Spirit in the three accounts we will consider below is to protect the church from their schemes and maneuvers.

Elymas the Magician
Acts 13:4-12

First Mission Begins in Cyprus. [4]So they, sent forth by the holy Spirit, went down to Seleucia and from there sailed to Cyprus. [5]When they arrived in Salamis, they proclaimed the word of God in the Jewish synagogues. They had John also as their assistant. [6]When they had traveled through the whole island as far as Paphos, they met a magician named Bar-Jesus who was a Jewish false prophet. [7]He was with the proconsul Sergius Paulus, a man of intelligence, who had summoned Barnabas and Saul and wanted to hear the word of God. [8]But Elymas the magician (for that is what his name means) opposed them in an attempt to turn the proconsul away from the faith. [9]But Saul, also known as Paul, filled with the holy Spirit, looked intently at him [10]and said, "You son of the devil, you enemy of all that is right, full of every sort of deceit and fraud. Will you not stop twisting the straight paths of [the] Lord? [11]Even now the hand of the Lord is upon you. You will be blind, and unable to see the sun for a time." Immediately a dark mist fell upon him, and he went about seeking people to lead him by the hand. [12]When the proconsul saw what had happened, he came to believe, for he was astonished by the teaching about the Lord.

 The apostle Paul had two names: **Saul and Paul**. "Saul" was his Hebrew name. It associated him with King Saul who was also from the tribe of Benjamin (1 Sam 9:21; Phil 3:5). "Paul" is a Latin form of Saul. The book of Acts uses Saul until 13:9, where it indicates that the two names are interchangeable: "Saul, also known as Paul." From this point forward Acts refers to the apostle as Paul. Adopting a Latin version of his name allowed Paul to relate better to his Gentile audience. It also seems to be his personal preference. In all of his undisputed letters (those that scholars generally agree were written by Paul himself), he identifies himself as Paul.

When Barnabas and Paul come to Paphos, they meet a magician with two names: Bar-Jesus (v. 6) and Elymas (v. 8). The Greek word used for "magician" is *magos*. It carries a wider meaning than the modern term, which is largely limited to the performance of staged illusions. In the ancient world, a *magos* could be a seer, teacher, astrologer, soothsayer, wonder-worker, or a person of wisdom. Calling someone a *magos* did not imply that the person was a fake or an impostor. Matthew's Gospel, for example, positively presents the magi who visit the Christ child (2:1-12). But Luke does not leave any doubt about the character of Elymas. He was a "false prophet" (v. 6), opposed to the gospel and to God's Spirit.

Such an attitude is a serious problem in light of Elymas's position. Verse 7 says that he was "with" the proconsul Sergius Paulus, who wanted to hear the word of God. Here, the Greek word for "with" does not describe a loose connection, such as physical proximity. It indicates that Elymas was part of the entourage of Sergius Paulus, possibly a court astrologer who was consulted when crucial decisions were to be made. In such an influential position, his advice could inhibit the proconsul's acceptance of the gospel, and the text indicates this is precisely Elymas's intention (v. 8). Elymas must be removed from the equation, and this is exactly what Paul does. Filled with the Spirit, Paul looks at the magician and renames him. He is not Bar-Jesus ("son of Jesus," a common name at the time) but "son of the devil" (v. 10). He becomes blind and must be led about by others. The influence Elymas exercised over Sergius Paulus is eliminated, and the proconsul comes to believe in the gospel (v. 12). The Spirit has protected the church's mission by removing a powerful opponent who could have obstructed the gift of faith.

Contemporary Relevance: The story of the magician Elymas can be read as a warning against false attachments. Just as Sergius Paulus could not appreciate the truth of the gospel while he was under the sway of Elymas, we are unable to live our faith fully if we bind ourselves to forces that pull against it. Addictions to alcohol, overeating, or pornography will cloud our perception of God's will and our ability to follow God's word. Feeding anger or revenge will distort our ability to experience God's love and serve God's mission. We cannot follow the gospel with a false prophet influencing us. As harmful attachments encircle us, we must pray to the Spirit to set us free.

Simon the Magician
Acts 8:9-25

[9]A man named Simon used to practice magic in the city and astounded the people of Samaria, claiming to be someone great. [10]All of them, from the least to the greatest, paid attention to him, saying, "This man is the 'Power of God' that is called

'Great.'" [11]They paid attention to him because he had astounded them by his magic for a long time, [12]but once they began to believe Philip as he preached the good news about the kingdom of God and the name of Jesus Christ, men and women alike were baptized. [13]Even Simon himself believed and, after being baptized, became devoted to Philip; and when he saw the signs and mighty deeds that were occurring, he was astounded.

[14]Now when the apostles in Jerusalem heard that Samaria had accepted the word of God, they sent them Peter and John, [15]who went down and prayed for them, that they might receive the holy Spirit, [16]for it had not yet fallen upon any of them; they had only been baptized in the name of the Lord Jesus. [17]Then they laid hands on them and they received the holy Spirit.

[18]When Simon saw that the Spirit was conferred by the laying on of the apostles' hands, he offered them money [19]and said, "Give me this power too, so that anyone upon whom I lay my hands may receive the holy Spirit." [20]But Peter said to him, "May your money perish with you, because you thought that you could buy the gift of God with money. [21]You have no share or lot in this matter, for your heart is not upright before God. [22]Repent of this wickedness of yours and pray to the Lord that, if possible, your intention may be forgiven. [23]For I see that you are filled with bitter gall and are in the bonds of iniquity." [24]Simon said in reply, "Pray for me to the Lord, that nothing of what you have said may come upon me." [25]So when they had testified and proclaimed the word of the Lord, they returned to Jerusalem and preached the good news to many Samaritan villages.

Philip, Peter, and John also encounter a magician as they preach in Samaria. Simon is not presented as "false" like Elymas, but he certainly has a high opinion of himself.

Luke gives us some important details about this magician. Simon "claim[ed] to be someone great" (v. 9). He had "astounded" the people of Samaria with his magic for a long time (v. 11). He always received great reviews. All the people, from the least to the greatest, thought he was the power of God (v. 10). Simon, it seems, was no average magician. He was a phenomenon. There is little doubt that he was happy with his success. He had established a recognizable brand that provided him with a profitable living.

But then Philip shows up and puts Simon's marvels to shame. The people abandon Simon and are baptized (v. 12). Simon, who is in turn "astounded" by the signs and deeds of Philip, decides not to fight Philip but to join him (v. 13). If Philip has the stronger magic, Simon wants in. Simon, too, is baptized and begins to follow Philip. When he sees that Peter and John confer the Spirit by the laying on of hands, he wants to add that power to his routine—and he is willing to pay (vv. 18-19). Anything to get his face back up on the billboards.

It is here that Luke reveals Simon's sin. It is not simply thinking he can buy a new trick. Simon sins by presuming that the Spirit can become a component of his human enterprise, that God's power can be obtained at will and included in his business portfolio. Peter says it best: Simon thought he "could buy the gift of God" (v. 20). But a gift cannot be bought, only received. The Spirit of God cannot be controlled, only welcomed. To Simon's credit, when Peter admonishes him, he repents (v. 24). Simon's conversion seems genuine enough, but it was a hard lesson for him to learn. God's Spirit will not submit to human control or organization.

Contemporary Relevance: All of us have talents and abilities. Most of us work hard to develop them. This often results in personal and financial success. We raise a healthy family. We develop a robust network of friends. We begin or expand a profitable business. There is nothing wrong with taking pride in our accomplishments. We may even have the insight to thank God for making our work possible, to see what we have attained as blessings. But there is a difference between giving thanks and truly believing that God is responsible. There is always the danger that our faith and moments of gratitude simply become part of a strategy we control. We can go to church and say our prayers, but in our hearts, we remain in charge. God has a place, but we decide what it will be. God becomes one of the tools at our disposal to achieve the ends we desire.

In such circumstances, we fail with Simon. We see our relationship with God as a benefit that can be bought, owned, and assigned a purpose among our resources. The only response to such an attitude, as Simon discovered, is repentance. God is not one part of our life but its very foundation. Everything we have is gift. Our life, health, talents, efforts, and opportunities all come from God. We are to cooperate with what has been given, but God controls it all. This is what Simon failed to see. The power of the Spirit cannot be bought, because the Spirit already possesses all that we are.

The name of Simon, the magician of Acts 8:9-25, has become associated with a particular sin. **"Simony"** is the sin of buying or selling a spiritual office, act, or privilege. This sin was unknown in the early church when Christianity was a marginal movement without influence. But when Christianity became the official religion of the empire under Constantine in the fourth century CE, people became willing to pay for positions within the church that could lead to their economic advancement. The first prohibition against simony was issued by the Council of Chalcedon in 451 CE.

Ananias and Sapphira
Acts 5:1-11

[1]A man named Ananias, however, with his wife Sapphira, sold a piece of property. [2]He retained for himself, with his wife's knowledge, some of the purchase price, took the remainder, and put it at the feet of the apostles. [3]But Peter said, "Ananias, why has Satan filled your heart so that you lied to the holy Spirit and retained part of the price of the land? [4]While it remained unsold, did it not remain yours? And when it was sold, was it not still under your control? Why did you contrive this deed? You have lied not to human beings, but to God." [5]When Ananias heard these words, he fell down and breathed his last, and great fear came upon all who heard of it. [6]The young men came and wrapped him up, then carried him out and buried him.

[7]After an interval of about three hours, his wife came in, unaware of what had happened. [8]Peter said to her, "Tell me, did you sell the land for this amount?" She answered, "Yes, for that amount." [9]Then Peter said to her, "Why did you agree to test the Spirit of the Lord? Listen, the footsteps of those who have buried your husband are at the door, and they will carry you out." [10]At once, she fell down at his feet and breathed her last. When the young men entered they found her dead, so they carried her out and buried her beside her husband. [11]And great fear came upon the whole church and upon all who heard of these things.

The last narrative we will consider in which the Spirit protects the church is the shocking story of Ananias and Sapphira. Luke regularly presents a positive view of the early church. "The community of believers was of one heart and mind"; they did not claim any of their possessions as their own but held all in common, setting their wealth "at the feet of the apostles" to be distributed to those in need (Acts 4:32-35). The story of Ananias and Sapphira represents a stark departure from this practice of community sharing. Although Ananias and Sapphira simulate donating the profit from a sale of property to the church, they in fact conspire with each other to keep part of money for themselves (vv. 1-2). When Peter exposes the plan, the response is immediate: they both drop dead.

This story raises an array of questions. How did Peter uncover the deception? Why did a selfish act concerning property occasion such severe punishment? Why were Ananias and Sapphira not offered an opportunity to repent? Some of these concerns can be mitigated by recognizing that the story has been heavily shaped for dramatic effect. For example, this account has undoubtedly been influenced by the story of Achan in Joshua 7:1-26, where a deceitful retention of goods also leads to the death of the offending party. Luke intends to present a riveting story, and he succeeds admirably. The purpose of his story is to provide a moral message: deception has consequences.

The deception of Ananias and Sapphira is profound. They lie to the Holy Spirit (vv. 3, 8-9). What does Luke mean by this expression? The actions of Ananias and Sapphira disfigure what the Spirit is doing in the world. We have already seen how the major theme of Acts is the Spirit spreading the gospel through the church. The communal sharing of goods was a visible way for the church to testify to the Spirit's power. The deception of Ananias and Sapphira, then, was a direct attack upon the Spirit. Their sin was not so much about greed and possessions but about a denial of the Spirit's effectiveness in human hearts. For this reason, their sin was so serious and their punishment so swift.

Luke seems to be drawing a comparison between **Ananias and Judas**. Peter asks Ananias, "[W]hy has Satan filled your heart?" (5:3). In Luke's Gospel, Judas's betrayal of Jesus is attributed to Satan: "Then Satan entered into Judas . . . and he went to the chief priests and temple guards to discuss a plan for handing him [Jesus] over to them" (22:3-4). Also, just as Ananias's sin was associated with a piece of property, Judas used the money he received for betraying Jesus to buy a piece of land (Acts 1:18). Finally, both men die graphic and sudden deaths after their sins are exposed—Ananias immediately "fell down and breathed his last" at Peter's feet (5:5); and Judas, after purchasing the parcel of land, "[fell] headlong" and "burst open in the middle" so that "all his insides spilled out" (1:18).

Contemporary Relevance: The story of Ananias and Sapphira is about a lie. We often assume that lies are small failings, discrepancies about the truth regarding a person or situation. But we should never underestimate the power of a lie. Disagreements can be resolved, hurts can be healed, progress can be made as long as people can agree on what is real. When

Engraving of Ananias and Sapphira

the truth is purposefully distorted, the human community fails. When deceit is introduced into a family, church, or political system, it undercuts the ability to move forward. When lies are accepted as reality, hope dies. We no longer have the capacity to communicate, compromise, or decide in an informed manner. We lose the common ground on which we live.

We believe that the goal of the Spirit is to create justice, peace, and truth within the human community. Therefore, to choose duplicity is to obstruct the work of God. To intentionally put forward a lie as the truth is a sin against the Holy Spirit and should not be taken lightly. Just ask Ananias and Sapphira—the consequences are fatal.

The Giving of the Spirit Cannot Be Controlled

As often as Acts presents the power of the Spirit, it does not always describe the giving of the Spirit in the same way. This is particularly true when we examine the manner in which Acts connects the Spirit to baptism and the laying on of hands by the apostles.

On Pentecost, Peter tells the crowd that if they repent and are baptized, they will receive "the gift of the holy Spirit" (2:38). This scene indicates that baptism imparts the power of the Spirit, an idea that is familiar to us. But in Acts 19:1-8, Paul visits Ephesus and finds some disciples of Jesus who are completely unaware of the Holy Spirit. Paul then baptizes them "in the name of the Lord Jesus" (v. 5), but they do not receive the Spirit until Paul lays his hands on them. Here, the Holy Spirit appears to come *after* baptism with the laying on of hands. The same is true in Acts 8:14-17, when Peter and John encounter disciples who were baptized in the name of Jesus but had not yet received the Holy Spirit. Peter and John lay hands on them, and the Spirit comes upon them. To complicate the issue, in Acts 10:44-49, Cornelius and his family listen to Peter preach, and the Holy Spirit is "poured out" upon them (v. 45). Witnessing the presence of the Spirit, Peter then orders them to be baptized in the name of Jesus. Here, the gift of the Spirit *precedes* baptism.

There is not a consistent relationship between the Spirit, baptism, and the laying on of hands in the book of Acts. One reason for this is historical. Catholic theology connects the activity of the Spirit with the sacraments. The gift of the Spirit is understood to be given in baptism, and a fuller share of the Spirit is instilled in confirmation through the laying on of hands. It took time, however, for the church to come to this full sacramental understanding. The varying ways Acts connects the Spirit to baptism and the laying on of hands might well reflect early, incomplete attempts to express the mystery of the Spirit's presence in the church's ritual actions.

This early inconsistency regarding the bestowal of the Spirit also suggests a deeper insight: the Spirit refuses to be pinned down. The Spirit remains free to act independently of the apostles' actions and intentions. Even though believers today can confidently name the sacramental ways in which the Spirit becomes present to them, the Spirit is not restrained by human understandings or rituals. The Spirit remains free and uncontrolled.

Contemporary Relevance: As baptized Christians, we believe we possess the Holy Spirit, and we certainly do. But the Spirit will never be restricted to who we are today. For years we may have faithfully participated in Mass and the sacraments. But the Spirit may instill in us a deep thirst for holiness that goes beyond our routine practices, and we may begin to take more time for personal prayer and spiritual reading. Perhaps we already have a rich spiritual life grounded in the Spirit. But the Spirit may spark our awareness of the profound need for justice in our world, and we may find ourselves increasingly active in efforts to eliminate poverty, racism, and the abuse of our environment.

Yes, we have been baptized, and we possess the Spirit, but the Spirit is not under our control. Like the apostles in Acts, who were startled to witness the Spirit move in ways and among people they did not expect, we should remember that not even a sacrament fully contains God's Spirit. The Spirit remains free to prod us, shape us, and re-create us in surprising ways so that we may become ever more authentic disciples of Jesus.

The Spirit Prepares Us for Suffering

Throughout Acts, Paul is presented as the primary missionary of the gospel, expanding church communities under the guidance of the Holy Spirit. Acts locates the end of Paul's missionary endeavors in the seaport city of Miletus. In this scene, Paul has decided he must travel to Jerusalem, where he knows imprisonment awaits. He calls the elders from Ephesus to meet him and delivers a lengthy and deeply personal farewell speech:

Acts 20:17-38

Paul's Farewell Speech at Miletus. [17]From Miletus he had the presbyters of the church at Ephesus summoned. [18]When they came to him, he addressed them, "You know how I lived among you the whole time from the day I first came to the province of Asia. [19]I served the Lord with all humility and with the tears and trials that came to me because of the plots of the Jews, [20]and I did not at all shrink from telling you what was for your benefit, or from teaching you in public or in your homes. [21]I earnestly bore witness for both Jews and Greeks to repentance before God and to faith in our Lord Jesus. [22]But now, compelled by the Spirit, I am going to Jerusalem. What will happen to me there I do not know, [23]except that in one city after another the holy Spirit has been warning me that imprisonment and hardships await me. [24]Yet I consider life of no importance to me, if only I may finish my course and the ministry that I received from the Lord Jesus, to bear witness to the gospel of God's grace.

[25]"But now I know that none of you to whom I preached the kingdom during my travels will ever see my face again. [26]And so I solemnly declare to you this day that I am not responsible for the blood of any of you, [27]for I did not shrink from proclaiming to you the entire plan of God. [28]Keep watch over yourselves and over the whole flock of which the holy Spirit has appointed you overseers, in which you tend the church of God that he acquired with his own blood. [29]I know that after my departure savage wolves will come among you, and they will not spare the flock. [30]And from your own group, men will come forward perverting the truth to draw the disciples away after them. [31]So be vigilant and remember that for three years, night and day, I unceasingly admonished each of you with tears. [32]And now I commend you to God and to that gracious word of his that can build you up and give you the inheritance among all who are consecrated. [33]I have never wanted anyone's silver or gold or clothing. [34]You know well that these very hands have served my needs and my companions. [35]In every way I have shown you that by hard work of that sort we must help the weak, and keep in mind the words of the Lord Jesus who himself said, 'It is more blessed to give than to receive.'"

[36]When he had finished speaking he knelt down and prayed with them all. [37]They were all weeping loudly as they threw their arms around Paul and kissed him, [38]for they were deeply distressed that he had said that they would never see his face again. Then they escorted him to the ship.

Paul's farewell speech is both sad and ominous. Paul testifies to the authenticity of his mission. He has borne witness "to repentance before God and to faith in our Lord Jesus" (v. 21). But the remainder of his life will include another kind of witness. He will no longer travel freely, founding new churches and expanding the community of believers. Instead, the last years of Paul's life will be comprised of confinement and suffering. As painful as those years may be, they are not accidental. His journey to Jerusalem is "compelled by the Spirit" (v. 22). Indeed, he tells the elders that he has known his future for some time. Although the particulars are not clear, Paul says that "in one city after another the holy Spirit has been warning me that imprisonment and hardships await me" (v. 23).

 Paul concludes his speech in Miletus with a saying of Jesus: **"It is more blessed to give than to receive"** (v. 35). At this key moment, as he draws his ministry to a close, Paul's last words are not his own but those of the Lord. Interestingly, as popular and well-known as this saying is, it occurs nowhere in the Gospels but is only preserved here in the book of Acts.

As Paul continues his journey to Jerusalem, the warnings of the Holy Spirit continue. When his boat stops in Tyre, disciples there warn him "through the Spirit" of the danger of continuing his voyage (21:4). When he arrives at Caesarea, he stays with Philip. There the Spirit speaks to him again through the prophet Agabus:

Acts 21:10-14

¹⁰We had been there several days when a prophet named Agabus came down from Judea. ¹¹He came up to us, took Paul's belt, bound his own feet and hands with it, and said, "Thus says the holy Spirit: This is the way the Jews will bind the owner of this belt in Jerusalem, and they will hand him over to the Gentiles." ¹²When we heard this, we and the local residents begged him not to go up to Jerusalem. ¹³Then Paul replied, "What are you doing, weeping and breaking my heart? I am prepared not only to be bound but even to die in Jerusalem for the name of the Lord Jesus." ¹⁴Since he would not be dissuaded we let the matter rest, saying, "The Lord's will be done."

The warning of the Holy Spirit through the words and action of Agabus are clear: Paul will be handed over to the Romans and will die at their hands. The remainder of Acts bears this out. Paul is arrested in Jerusalem (21:33), imprisoned in Caesarea for two years (24:22-27), and sent to Rome when he appeals to the emperor (25:12). Acts ends with Paul under house arrest in Rome, awaiting his trial (28:16). Although this ending may seem incomplete, it suits the missionary trajectory of Acts. The preaching of the gospel has reached "the ends of the earth" (1:8).

What does Paul's ominous journey to Rome tell us about the Holy Spirit? The Spirit's frequent warnings in Acts are not intended simply to inform Paul. They also remind him of the Spirit's presence. The Holy Spirit cares for the apostle and will stand with him when he suffers. To make this truth clear, Luke carefully conforms Paul's suffering to that of Jesus. Agabus declares that Paul will be handed "over to the Gentiles" (v. 11). This echoes the prediction of Jesus' passion in Luke 18:32: "He will be handed over to the Gentiles." When Paul states that he is prepared not only to be bound but to die for the name of Jesus, the disciples around him accept this, saying, "The Lord's will be done" (vv. 13-14). These same words are spoken by Jesus on the Mount of Olives before his death: "not my will but yours be done" (Luke 22:42). The Spirit's warnings to Paul both prepare and assure him. As a witness to the gospel, Paul can depend upon the Spirit to support him just as God's Spirit supported Jesus during his passion.

Contemporary Relevance: Throughout our lives we receive premonitions of what is to come. Not all our premonitions are positive. A congenital heart problem in one of our children suggests that serious health issues will follow. A significant pattern of anger or selfishness in our spouse forewarns of a difficult or even broken relationship ahead. A recurring pain in our hip or knee hints that additional deterioration may set in as we age. We never know with certainty, but we have been warned.

As people of faith, we can accept such warnings as the voice of the Spirit. It is a voice that does not coddle us. We live in an imperfect world where bad things happen. But because we believe with Luke that the Spirit who dwells within us is the Spirit of God, because we trust that the one who speaks to us is the one who cares for us, we are able to hear a promise within the warning. We are able to recognize God's commitment to remain with us, to provide the strength that will allow us to stay the course and bear the pain that comes to us. And when we understand that the Spirit of God will always stand with us, we can say, with Jesus, Paul, and every true disciple, "Thy will be done."

Luke dramatizes **Paul's journey to Rome** with a lengthy account of his sea voyage. Taking up the better part of two chapters (27:1–28:16), the trip begins in Caesarea and ends in Italy. It includes a storm and a shipwreck, a winter in Malta, and the nearly fatal bite of a viper. The journey is modeled on similar voyages found in Greek literature, but its theological purpose is clear: the Spirit continues to carry Paul and the gospel he proclaims to "the ends of the earth."

EXPLORING LESSON FIVE

1. In what sense can Acts be called "The Book of the Holy Spirit"? How would you express the central message of Acts? How is this message connected to the geographical trajectory of the narrative?

_____

_____

_____

_____

_____

_____

2. How does Luke's brief and somewhat restrained description of the Pentecost scene serve his larger theological purpose (Acts 2:1-13)? How have you experienced the Spirit acting as warmth, light, or burning?

_____

_____

_____

_____

_____

_____

3. Give several examples of how the Spirit permeates the life of the early church in the book of Acts. What is Luke trying to communicate with such frequent mentions of the Spirit?

_____

_____

_____

_____

_____

4. What is a *magos* in the book of Acts, and are such individuals presented positively or negatively (see commentary on Acts 13:4-12)? What does Luke communicate by contrasting *magi* with the work of the Spirit?

_____

_____

_____

_____

_____

5. Luke presents the magician Elymas as a force opposed to the gospel (Acts 13:4-12). Paul defeats the threat Elymas poses. What forces do you think threaten the gospel in our world today? How might we effectively take steps against them?

_____

_____

_____

_____

_____

6. This lesson suggests that the story of Ananias and Sapphira is a moral tale meant to demonstrate that deception has consequences (Acts 5:1-11). How prevalent are lies in our culture today? Who is using them and for what purposes? As a Christian, how do you feel you are called to oppose the power of a lie?

_____

_____

_____

_____

_____

7. Acts connects faith, baptism, and the laying on of hands with God's Spirit in different ways (see section "The Giving of the Spirit Cannot Be Controlled"). This lesson suggests that these variations emphasize the freedom of God's Spirit. Has God's Spirit ever led you in directions you did not expect or even appreciate? Can you share an experience of the Spirit acting freely in your life?

_____

_____

_____

_____

_____

8. In the final chapters of Acts, Paul is warned repeatedly of future suffering. Has the Spirit ever warned you about difficulties to come? How does Paul's commitment to journey on to Jerusalem help you reflect on these difficulties?

_____

_____

_____

_____

_____

9. What story or insight from this chapter stands out as you look back on what you have read and learned? What does this story or insight tell you about the Holy Spirit and about the church?

_____

_____

_____

_____

_____

_____

CLOSING PRAYER

Prayer

"Repent and be baptized, every one of you, in the name of Jesus Christ for the forgiveness of your sins; and you will receive the gift of the holy Spirit." (Acts 2:38)

Lord Jesus, you promised to send the Paraclete, your Spirit, to be with us always. May your Spirit dwell with us in the heart of the church, inspiring us to live and share the good news of your life, death, and resurrection. May we never be guilty of quenching or trying to control your Spirit, but may we live in openness to the transforming power of your presence. Today we pray for our church, especially . . .

LESSON SIX

The Holy Spirit at the End of Time

Begin your personal study and group discussion with a simple and sincere prayer such as:

Prayer

Spirit of God, you breathe life into human beings and into your Word. Fill us with your presence as we spend time with your Word and one another. Re-create us and sustain us day by day.

Read pages 94–104, Lesson Six.

Respond to the questions on pages 105–107, Exploring Lesson Six.

The Closing Prayer on page 108 is for your personal use and may be used at the end of group discussion.

THE HOLY SPIRIT AT THE END OF TIME

The First Letter to the Thessalonians, written by the apostle Paul around 51 CE, is the earliest work of the New Testament. Paul's writings are essential to our understanding of Christian faith and practice. They provide a witness to the gospel message that is significantly earlier than the first written Gospel (ca. 68 CE) and other New Testament works such as Luke's Acts of the Apostles (ca. 85 CE).

Thirteen letters of the New Testament are associated with Paul. However, there is an ongoing debate over which letters were actually written by him. After Paul's death, other authors who respected Paul composed works and attributed them to him. Therefore, the New Testament contains some letters authored by Paul and others that simply bear his name. There is, however, a strong consensus among scholars that seven New Testament letters were undoubtedly written by Paul: Romans, First and Second Corinthians, Galatians, Philippians, First Thessalonians, and Philemon. This lesson will present Paul's understanding of the Holy Spirit as reflected in those seven letters. Such an approach is appropriate, not only because Paul's letters are the earliest recorded witness to the gospel of Jesus Christ, but also because Paul's belief in the Spirit carries a deep relevance for contemporary faith.

The word "gospel" comes from a Greek word meaning "good news." It was not originally a religious term but was used in the secular culture of the ancient world to announce a spectacular event, such as a victory in battle or the birth of an emperor. Paul uses the term extensively throughout his letters. For Paul, the "gospel" is the ultimate good news: God's plan to re-create the world has begun in the resurrection of Jesus. The term continued to be used by early Christians and eventually was applied to the four canonical writings that recount the ministry, death, and resurrection of Jesus: Matthew, Mark, Luke, and John.

Paul's Gospel

To fully appreciate Paul's view of the Spirit, we must first understand Paul's gospel, his understanding of Christ's role in the plan of salvation. Fortunately, there is a remarkable passage in 1 Corinthians 15 that clearly lays out Paul's viewpoint. The passage is lengthy and does not explicitly mention the Spirit, yet without it, the role of the Spirit in Paul's thought cannot be grasped:

---

1 Corinthians 15:12-28

Results of Denial. [12]But if Christ is preached as raised from the dead, how can some among you say there is no resurrection of the dead? [13]If there is no resurrection of the dead, then neither has Christ been raised. [14]And if Christ has not been raised, then empty [too] is our preaching; empty, too, your faith. [15]Then we are also false witnesses to God, because we testified against God that he raised Christ, whom he did not raise if in fact the dead are not raised. [16]For if the dead are not raised, neither has Christ been raised, [17]and if Christ has not been raised, your faith is vain; you are still in your sins. [18]Then those who have fallen asleep in Christ have perished. [19]If for this life only we have hoped in Christ, we are the most pitiable people of all.

Christ the Firstfruits. [20]But now Christ has been raised from the dead, the firstfruits of those who have fallen asleep. [21]For since death came through a human being, the resurrection of the dead came also through a human being. [22]For just as in Adam all die, so too in Christ shall all be brought to life, [23]but each one in proper order: Christ the firstfruits; then, at his coming, those who belong to Christ; [24]then comes the end, when he hands over the kingdom to his God and Father, when he has destroyed every sovereignty and every authority and power. [25]For he must reign until he has put all his enemies under his feet. [26]The last enemy to be destroyed is death, [27]for "he subjected everything under his feet." But when it says that everything has been subjected, it is clear that it excludes the one who subjected everything to him. [28]When everything is subjected to him, then the Son himself will [also] be subjected to the one who subjected everything to him, so that God may be all in all.

Paul does not view Jesus' resurrection as an end in itself. It is a crucial part of a larger plan by God to eliminate evil from the world. Paul makes this point by calling Jesus "the firstfruits of those who have fallen asleep" (v. 20). The term "firstfruits" is an agricultural image. Firstfruits are the first part of the crop to be harvested and are therefore inseparably linked to the remaining harvest that will follow. Paul uses this image to connect Jesus' resurrection with a reality that is to follow it—the resurrection of all who believe in Christ. To illustrate this connection, Paul provides a simple timeline of events in which Jesus' resurrection is only one step: "For just as in Adam all die, so too in Christ shall all be brought to life, but each one in proper order: Christ the firstfruits; then, at his coming, those who belong to Christ" (vv. 22-23). The entire harvest will not be complete until all those who belong to Christ share in a similar resurrection at his return.

Paul has now connected Christ's resurrection to the resurrection of the dead. He then makes them both part of a still greater plan.

This is the earliest and clearest expression of what the gospel, the good news, is about. It is therefore the earliest witness of what *Christianity* is about. Most Christians know the importance of Easter as the celebration of Jesus' resurrection from the dead. Christ's resurrection *is* the good news. Yet when Christians are asked *why* Christ's resurrection is good news, their response is often tentative and unfocused. This is discouraging. Something as central as the resurrection should be clearly understood.

Paul provides the understanding we need in the passage above from 1 Corinthians. Some Christians in Corinth had apparently concluded that the resurrection of believers who had died was not important or possible (v. 12). Paul hears of this and writes to correct what he feels is a serious misconception. He asserts that the resurrection of those who have died is directly connected to Jesus' resurrection. To deny either resurrection is to render the gospel and faith in Christ "empty" and useless (vv. 13-19). Paul then explains why.

Statue of St. Paul at St. Peter's Square, Vatican City

When the dead are raised, the end will come. Then Christ will destroy "every sovereignty and every authority and power" (v. 24). Paul insists that God intends not only to save believers but to eradicate all evil from the world. The sovereignties, authorities, and powers of which Paul speaks are not political entities. They are the spiritual forces of evil that still dominate human existence. These are the "enemies" that Christ will destroy when he returns (v. 25). Paul has in mind such "enemies" as injustice, war, sickness, hunger, and hatred. These are only some of the evils contrary to God's will, but God intends to destroy every one of them through Christ. The greatest enemy is saved for last: even death will be destroyed (v. 26).

Paul's gospel asserts that God has embarked on a final, cosmic project that involves not only Jesus' resurrection but the resurrection of the dead and the re-creation of the world. In fact, God intends to extend goodness to all that exists, establishing the perfection that was God's goal at creation. All that is evil will be destroyed. All that will remain is what God desires. Paul proclaims this truth as he concludes his timeline. When Christ returns, he will submit all things to God "so that God may be all in all" (v. 28). This is what Christianity is about. This is why Jesus' resurrection is good news for the Corinthians and for Christians today: God will be all in all. Jesus' resurrection has already begun to re-create the world and remove every evil that disfigures what God has made.

Where do Christians find themselves in the gospel that Paul proclaims? The answer is in the middle and in between. The first part of God's plan has been realized, yet the remaining part must still occur. Jesus has been raised up, and with his resurrection God has irrevocably begun the destruction of all evil. Yet many evils remain in the world. Violence and injustice are prevalent. Suffering, hurt, and disease still characterize human life. Therefore, Christians await the completion of God's victory in Christ. Their salvation is "already" but "not yet." Believers find themselves in the middle of God's plan, caught "in between" a present existence that is coming to an end and the kingdom of God that is not yet fully established.

Paul's gospel places Christians in a necessary tension between what they already possess and what they still await. This tension in the gospel must be maintained. If it is relaxed, the gospel is distorted. On one hand, focusing exclusively on what has already been accomplished in Christ's resurrection can deafen Christians to the imperfection of the world and the evil that continues to oppress humanity and diminish human life. On the other hand, focusing only on present evils erodes the hope that flows from Christ's resurrection. What makes Christians unique is that they believe not only that God will save the world but that God has definitively begun to do so in Christ Jesus. Therefore, followers of Jesus must live in a holy tension, looking backward and believing in Christ's resurrection, and look-

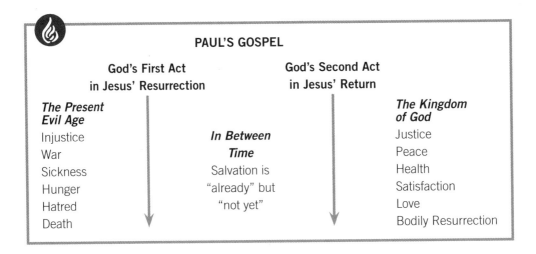

PAUL'S GOSPEL

	God's First Act **in Jesus' Resurrection**	**God's Second Act** **in Jesus' Return**	
The Present *Evil Age*			*The Kingdom* *of God*
Injustice		*In Between*	Justice
War		*Time*	Peace
Sickness		Salvation is	Health
Hunger		"already" but	Satisfaction
Hatred		"not yet"	Love
Death			Bodily Resurrection

ing forward in the hope that what God has begun will invariably be completed.

Contemporary Relevance: We all experience evil in our lives. Whether our lives have been touched by sickness, betrayal, depression, or death, the forces of evil are real and personal. Christ's resurrection assures us that God opposes the evil we experience. God intends to destroy every evil, but that has "not yet" been accomplished. Therefore, as we wait for God's final victory, we accept the reality of evil, knowing that we do not suffer alone. We join our suffering to the pain of the world. We wait with all creation for the glory that is to come.

But even as we own the "not yet" of salvation, we gain strength from what has already taken place. Christ is risen! Our faith tells us this is true. Because death has been destroyed in him, the days of death and every other evil are numbered. Even in our darkest moments, we can rally our hope because we know that the timeline of salvation has begun to unfold. Christians should be the most hopeful of all people because we not only believe that the triumph of God has been promised to us but that it has already begun. As we stand in the "in between" of God's plan, we look forward to what is to come, to that day when God will be all in all. What has happened will invariably lead to what is promised. This is why Jesus' resurrection is the gospel—good news for our lives.

The remainder of this lesson will examine the role of the Spirit across the axis of the "already" and the "not yet." Christians already possess and live according to the Spirit. The same Spirit, however, serves as the promise of the new creation that has not yet arrived.

Already: Christians Possess the Spirit

The Spirit of God makes faith in Jesus possible, and because of Jesus' resurrection, those who believe in Christ already possess the Spirit. Paul reminds the Thessalonians, "For our gospel did not come to you in word alone, but also in power and in the holy Spirit and [with] much conviction" (1 Thess 1:5). Paul tells the Corin-

thians that their ability to believe is a gift of the Spirit. They cannot call out Jesus' name without the Spirit: "And no one can say, 'Jesus is Lord,' except by the holy Spirit" (1 Cor 12:3).

Paul's letter to the Galatians is also clear that those who believe already possess God's Spirit. After Paul founded the church in Galatia, opponents of Paul arrived and argued that his gospel was faulty. Although Paul had brought the Galatians to faith in Jesus, his opponents insisted that the new believers must be circumcised and follow the Jewish law. Paul hears of this development and writes to the Galatians in anger:

Galatians 3:1-5

Justification by Faith. [1]O stupid Galatians! Who has bewitched you, before whose eyes Jesus Christ was publicly portrayed as crucified? [2]I want to learn only this from you: did you receive the Spirit from works of the law, or from faith in what you heard? [3]Are you so stupid? After beginning with the Spirit, are you now ending with the flesh? [4]Did you experience so many things in vain?—if indeed it was in vain. [5]Does, then, the one who supplies the Spirit to you and works mighty deeds among you do so from works of the law or from faith in what you heard?

Although Paul's main concern in this passage is to refute the claims of his opponents, his argument reveals that when the Galatians accepted the gospel, they received the Spirit as well (v. 2). Paul points to "mighty deeds" as signs of the Spirit's presence among them. He does not describe what these deeds were, but he reminds the Galatians that such deeds assure them that they possess the Spirit who was "supplie[d]" by God (v. 5). Paul's argument is from experience. He wants the Galatians to remember how their faith began, how they received the Spirit. He is adamant that faith in the gospel and the gift of the Spirit are inextricably linked. They must not let that originating gift of the Spirit go.

Contemporary Relevance: Most of us can point to an experience when we knew that God's Spirit was with us. If we came to faith as an adult, we can recall the power of our initiation. If we were born into a faith community, we can identify moments when the Spirit's presence was palpable: our first communion, marriage, or the birth of a child. We know the Spirit is with us in such moments. We must remember them because they ground our relationship with Christ. We cannot be like the Galatians who forgot where they began and drifted toward other beliefs and practices. God's Spirit has founded our faith. We must remain in what we have received.

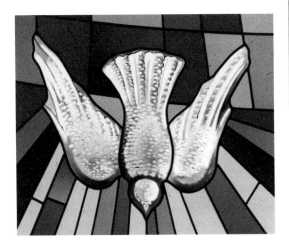

In 1 Corinthians 6:19, Paul uses a vivid image to describe the possession of the Spirit. Arguing against immorality, he says, "Do you not know that your body is a temple of the holy Spirit within you, whom you have from God, and that you are not your own?" Earlier in the letter, he argues, "Do you not know that you are the temple of God, and that the Spirit of God dwells in you? If anyone destroys God's temple, God will destroy that person; for the temple of God, which you are, is holy" (3:16-17). Believers, then, are holy temples, sacred places in which the Spirit of God dwells.

The Spirit who dwells in believers also allows them to know God. In 1 Corinthians 2:9-13, Paul begins with a quote inspired by Isaiah 64:3 and then describes the action of the Spirit:

---

1 Corinthians 2:9-13

⁹But as it is written:
"What eye has not seen, and ear has not heard,
and what has not entered the human heart,
what God has prepared for those who love him,"
¹⁰this God has revealed to us through the Spirit.

For the Spirit scrutinizes everything, even the depths of God. ¹¹Among human beings, who knows what pertains to a person except the spirit of the person that is within? Similarly, no one knows what pertains to God except the Spirit of God. ¹²We have not received the spirit of the world but the Spirit that is from God, so that we may understand the things freely given us by God. ¹³And we speak about them not with words taught by human wisdom, but with words taught by the Spirit, describing spiritual realities in spiritual terms.

Paul is well aware that God is totally different from us. Human insight can never grasp God's being. Human efforts alone could never connect or communicate with God. The Spirit, however, allows believers to know God. The Spirit alone knows the depths of God (vv. 10-11). Because believers have God's Spirit, they can partially grasp what God is doing and can speak about God in words taught by the Spirit (vv. 12-13). The Spirit, then, serves as a kind of translator, bridging the vast difference between God and humanity. God and God's ways can never be fully understood, but the Spirit provides believers with a connection that makes a relationship with God possible.

Paul also believes that the Spirit enables followers of Christ to serve others, and he ascribes the success of his mission to the Spirit. His role as apostle to the Gentiles has been directed and sanctified by the Holy Spirit (Rom 15:16, 19), and his ability to bring faith to the Corinthians results from the Spirit's power:

2 Corinthians 3:1-6

[1]Are we beginning to commend ourselves again? Or do we need, as some do, letters of recommendation to you or from you? [2]You are our letter, written on our hearts, known and read by all, [3]shown to be a letter of Christ administered by us, written not in ink but by the Spirit of the living God, not on tablets of stone but on tablets that are hearts of flesh.

[4]Such confidence we have through Christ toward God. [5]Not that of ourselves we are qualified to take credit for anything as coming from us; rather, our qualification comes from God, [6]who has indeed qualified us as ministers of a new covenant, not of letter but of spirit; for the letter brings death, but the Spirit gives life.

Romans 8:5-13

[5]For those who live according to the flesh are concerned with the things of the flesh, but those who live according to the spirit with the things of the spirit. [6]The concern of the flesh is death, but the concern of the spirit is life and peace. [7]For the concern of the flesh is hostility toward God; it does not submit to the law of God, nor can it; [8]and those who are in the flesh cannot please God. [9]But you are not in the flesh; on the contrary, you are in the spirit, if only the Spirit of God dwells in you. Whoever does not have the Spirit of Christ does not belong to him. [10]But if Christ is in you, although the body is dead because of sin, the spirit is alive because of righteousness. [11]If the Spirit of the one who raised Jesus from the dead dwells in you, the one who raised Christ from the dead will give life to your mortal bodies also, through his Spirit that dwells in you. [12]Consequently, brothers, we are not debtors to the flesh, to live according to the flesh. [13]For if you live according to the flesh, you will die, but if by the spirit you put to death the deeds of the body, you will live.

Preachers of Paul's day carried written credentials that were meant to validate their qualifications. Paul argues that he needs no such documents. The Corinthians themselves are his credentials. Their faith in Christ is the visible sign of the success of his ministry (v. 2). Their faith does not come from Paul but from God (v. 5). The faith of the Corinthians was written by the Spirit, who inscribed it in their hearts (v. 3). Paul is the model for Christian ministry. Like him, followers of Christ are not the source of their own effectiveness. Only the Spirit gives life (v. 6).

Already: Christians Live According to the Spirit

Throughout Paul's letters, he asserts that because Christians possess the Spirit, they should live according to the Spirit. He insists that the moral choices of his communities be guided by the Spirit. He tells the Galatians, "If we live in the Spirit, let us also follow the Spirit. Let us not be conceited, provoking one another, envious of one another" (Gal 5:25-26). Paul expands this perspective in Romans:

To follow Paul's argument in this passage, the meaning of "flesh" must be correctly understood. The word "flesh" translates the Greek word *sarx*, which has a technical meaning for Paul. "Flesh" here does not refer to the human body. It describes the entire human person insofar as that person is positioned against God's Spirit. Flesh and Spirit are opposed to each other, but the difference is not the opposition between the material and the spiritual. Flesh and Spirit are to be identified with the two ages of Paul's gospel. Flesh refers to the entire human person who belongs to the present age, where evil and opposition to God still exist. Spirit refers to the entire human person who belongs to the age to come, God's kingdom.

As we have already noted, the Christian believer lives "in between" these two ages. Therefore, in making moral choices, a believer is influenced by both. On the one hand, Paul tells the Romans that they are "not in the flesh" (v. 9). In other words, they are not opposed to God; they possess God's Spirit. Therefore, they already participate in the age to come. On the other hand, their choices can be influenced by the present age. They can choose to live "according to the flesh" (v. 5). Paul equates the believer's mortal body with the present age because, in the present age, the body is still influenced by sin (v. 10). But sinfulness is not the destiny of the body. At the resurrection on the last day, believers will receive a new glorified body through the Spirit (v. 11). These glorified, immortal bodies will participate fully in the kingdom of God.

In the Apostles' Creed, we profess: "I believe in **the resurrection of the body**." The *Catechism* relies on Paul's language from Romans 8:11 in its explanation of this credal statement, saying that it "means not only that the immortal *soul* will live on after death, but that even our 'mortal *body*' will come to life again" (*CCC* 990; emphasis added).

Believers, then, are pulled in two directions, corresponding to the two ages between which they stand. When Paul tells his communities to walk in the Spirit, he is directing them to make choices aligned to the age to come, an age of "life and peace," rather than to the present age that is characterized by "death" (v. 6). Christians are not to live according to the flesh but according to the Spirit (vv. 12-13).

Paul employs this same contrast in Galatians:

Galatians 5:16-23

[16]I say, then: live by the Spirit and you will certainly not gratify the desire of the flesh. [17]For the flesh has desires against the Spirit, and the Spirit against the flesh; these are opposed to each other,

---

so that you may not do what you want. [18]But if you are guided by the Spirit, you are not under the law. [19]Now the works of the flesh are obvious: immorality, impurity, licentiousness, [20]idolatry, sorcery, hatreds, rivalry, jealousy, outbursts of fury, acts of selfishness, dissensions, factions, [21]occasions of envy, drinking bouts, orgies, and the like. I warn you, as I warned you before, that those who do such things will not inherit the kingdom of God. [22]In contrast, the fruit of the Spirit is love, joy, peace, patience, kindness, generosity, faithfulness, [23]gentleness, self-control. Against such there is no law.

Here again the believer is poised between two ages, two ways of life. Paul offers qualities that describe what life in the flesh and life in the Spirit entail. The two lists are not exhaustive. Such lists of vices and virtues were a common literary device in the ancient world and were often used for illustration and emphasis. Paul himself offers different renderings of such lists in Romans 1:29-31 and 1 Corinthians 6:9-10. Tradition, however, has taken up Paul's positive qualities in Galatians 5:22-23 and made them a defined part of Christian spirituality, calling them "the fruits of the Spirit." They allow believers to recognize how someone guided by the Spirit should live.

The *Catechism* names **three more fruits of the Spirit** than are found in Galatians 5:22-23. The additional fruits (generosity, modesty, and chastity) arise from a variation in an ancient Latin translation of the Bible (the Vulgate). The difference in numbers should not disturb us. The list that Paul provides is not meant to be exhaustive. What is important is the future thrust of the qualities. As the *Catechism* clearly states, these "perfections" that the Holy Spirit forms in us are "the first fruits of eternal glory" (1832).

Already: The Spirit and the Body of Christ

One of the most compelling images in Paul's letters is that of the Body of Christ in 1 Corinthians 12. This image reveals multiple dimensions of God's Spirit:

1 Corinthians 12:4-27

[4]There are different kinds of spiritual gifts but the same Spirit; [5]there are different forms of service but the same Lord; [6]there are different workings but the same God who produces all of them in everyone. [7]To each individual the manifestation of the Spirit is given for some benefit. [8]To one is given through the Spirit the expression of wisdom; to another the expression of knowledge according to the same Spirit; [9]to another faith by the same Spirit; to another gifts of healing by the one Spirit; [10]to another mighty deeds; to another prophecy; to another discernment of spirits; to another varieties of tongues; to another interpretation of tongues. [11]But one and the same Spirit produces all of these, distributing them individually to each person as he wishes.

One Body, Many Parts. [12]As a body is one though it has many parts, and all the parts of the body, though many, are one body, so also Christ. [13]For in one Spirit we were all baptized into one body, whether Jews or Greeks, slaves or free persons, and we were all given to drink of one Spirit.

[14]Now the body is not a single part, but many. [15]If a foot should say, "Because I am not a hand I do not belong to the body," it does not for this reason belong any less to the body. [16]Or if an ear should say, "Because I am not an eye I do not belong to the body," it does not for this reason belong any less to the body. [17]If the whole body were an eye, where would the hearing be? If the whole body were hearing, where would the sense of smell be? [18]But as it is, God placed the parts, each one of them, in the body as he intended. [19]If they were all one part, where would the body be? [20]But as it is, there are many parts, yet one body. [21]The eye cannot say to the hand, "I do not need you," nor again the head to the feet, "I do not need you." [22]Indeed, the parts of the body that seem to be weaker are all the more necessary, [23]and those parts of the body that we consider less honorable we surround with greater honor, and our less presentable parts are treated with greater propriety, [24]whereas our more presentable parts do not need this. But God has so constructed the body as to give greater honor to a part that is without it, [25]so that there may be no division in the body, but that the parts may have the same concern for one another. [26]If [one] part suffers, all the parts suffer with it; if one part is honored, all the parts share its joy.

Application to Christ. [27]Now you are Christ's body, and individually parts of it.

Through the image of the body, Paul presents the community of believers, the church, as the living presence of Christ, a single organism animated by God's Spirit. Through baptism the Spirit has formed believers into the body and has become their "drink" (v. 13). The Spirit bestows differing gifts to each member of the body for the benefit of all (vv. 7-11). The Spirit is the force for unity in the body because although the gifts differ, the Spirit is one (v. 4).

Using the **image of the body** as a metaphor is not unique to Paul. The body was commonly used in the ancient world as a literary image for society. Examples of this usage can be found in the writings of Plato, Cicero, Seneca, and the Roman senator, Menenius Agrippa. The common point was that, like a human body, some members of society were more important than others, and it was therefore necessary to subordinate certain members of society to other members. Paul departs from this thinking. Rather than calling for a subordination of some members, he insists that all the parts of the body should care for each other.

Several Christian beliefs are held together in Paul's image of the Body of Christ. First, every member of Christ's body is gifted. The Spirit assures this (v. 11). Second, the gifts of the body are diverse (vv. 4-6). Paul enumerates some of these gifts as wisdom, knowledge, faith, healing, mighty deeds, prophecy, discernment of spirits, variety of tongues, and interpretation of tongues (vv. 8-10). Third, the parts of the body are not the same. Different parts have different functions, and some parts "seem to be weaker" and "less honorable" (v. 22-23). Fourth, all parts of the body are necessary because they are all needed to form one body (vv. 12, 19, 22). Finally, the difference in parts is intended by God to engender unity in the body and care for the weaker parts (vv. 24-25). Through this complex interaction of parts and their unity across differences, Christ is made present in the world. God's Spirit animates the Body of Christ and guides its life.

Contemporary Relevance: Allow me to suggest two ways that Paul's understanding of the Body of Christ affects our lives.

1) *All of us are gifted.* Paul insists that if we belong to Christ, we have been given a gift. The Spirit has bestowed a gift to "each individual" (v. 7). There are times when we are tempted to question this assertion. There are days when we doubt our worth, wondering what we can contribute to the good of others. We may compare our gifts to those of others and find our own gifts lacking. After a devastating failure or loss, we can lose a sense of purpose and struggle to find a way forward. In such times, we need to remember that denying our giftedness contradicts the word of God. God has not just made us. God has gifted us. We may at times lose sight of our gifts, and occasionally we may discover new ones. But all of us have received abilities from God's Spirit, and the only way we can validate God's grace is to use them.

2) *The gifts of the Spirit are not equal, but they are all necessary.* Paul does not believe that all the gifts that comprise Christ's body are equal. In 1 Corinthians 12:28-30, he ranks the value of the gifts, putting apostles first and tongues last. He considers some gifts more important to Christ's body

than others. We can validate his perspective from our own experience. For example, the parish co-ordinator of religious formation has more influence over community life than the eight-year-old child making his or her first communion.

Such ranking of importance may run counter to our modern sensibilities. Paul, however, does propose a type of equality within the body. We are equal in that we are all necessary. Human nature assumes that because some are less gifted, they are less valuable. We are tempted to believe that we will move further ahead with a few strong players rather than with a multitude of the weak. Paul's view of the Body of Christ provides an alternate perspective. Each person is necessary because each person is a part of the body held together by the Spirit of God. The Spirit shows us that, through all our differences, we still need each other. Even though our abilities are not equal, our care for each other must be consistent (v. 25). Those who have been given the greater gifts are to be valued accordingly. But no person is expendable. No one can be left behind. In fact, every part of the body has a responsibility to care for those who are weaker (vv. 22-24). No one can say to another person, "I do not need you" (v. 21), because every person is a part of us.

Not Yet: The Spirit as Promise

Christians already possess God's Spirit. That gift also serves as a promise and pledge for the age to come. Paul sees the Spirit, already bestowed, as a "first installment," as he explains in 2 Corinthians 1:21-22: "But the one who gives us security with you in Christ and who anointed us is God; he has also put his seal upon us and given the Spirit in our hearts as a first installment." Paul repeats this expression in 2 Corinthians 5:5: "Now the one who has prepared us for this very thing is God, who has given us the Spirit as a first installment." Calling the Spirit a "first installment" gives a future thrust to Paul's understanding of the Spirit. The Spirit serves as a down payment or guarantee that the final victory of Christ will come.

Paul gives his fullest description of the Spirit's future role in Romans 8:

Romans 8:14-27

Children of God through Adoption. [14]For those who are led by the Spirit of God are children of God. [15]For you did not receive a spirit of slavery to fall back into fear, but you received a spirit of adoption, through which we cry, "*Abba*, Father!" [16]The Spirit itself bears witness with our spirit that we are children of God, [17]and if children, then heirs, heirs of God and joint heirs with Christ, if only we suffer with him so that we may also be glorified with him.

Destiny of Glory. [18]I consider that the sufferings of this present time are as nothing compared with the glory to be revealed for us. [19]For creation awaits with eager expectation the revelation of the children of God; [20]for creation was made subject to futility, not of its own accord but because of the one who subjected it, in hope [21]that creation itself would be set free from slavery to corruption and share in the glorious freedom of the children of God. [22]We know that all creation is groaning in labor pains even until now; [23]and not only that, but we ourselves, who have the firstfruits of the Spirit, we also groan within ourselves as we wait for adoption, the redemption of our bodies. [24]For in hope we were saved. Now hope that sees for itself is not hope. For who hopes for what one sees? [25]But if we hope for what we do not see, we wait with endurance.

[26]In the same way, the Spirit too comes to the aid of our weakness; for we do not know how to pray as we ought, but the Spirit itself intercedes with inexpressible groanings. [27]And the one who searches hearts knows what is the intention of the Spirit, because it intercedes for the holy ones according to God's will.

In this passage Paul begins by affirming the present identity of believers. They possess God's Spirit, and the Spirit "bears witness" that they are "children of God" (v. 16). Because they have "received a spirit of adoption," they are able to pray to God as "Abba, Father!" (v. 15; see also Gal 4:6). In verses 17-18, Paul pivots to the future. Because Christians are children, they are also heirs. The Spirit they already possess is the guarantee of glory to come. The "already" leads to the "not yet." The gift of the Spirit provides hope in the fulfillment of God's plan and is transforming believers in the promise of Christ's return. As Paul writes in 2 Corinthians 3:17-18, "Now the Lord is the Spirit, and where the Spirit of the Lord is, there is freedom. All of us, gazing with unveiled face on the glory of the Lord, are being transformed into the same image from glory to glory, as from the Lord who is the Spirit."

Paul then widens his perspective beyond individuals and the community of believers. Not only Christians but *all that has been created* awaits the glory that is to come (vv. 19-21). Paul uses birthing language to describe the experience of waiting "in between" the two ages of his gospel. Followers of Christ and all creation are "groaning in labor pains" (v. 22). Everything is caught up in the painful process of giving birth to the new age of God's kingdom. But Christians have hope because they already possess the "firstfruits of the Spirit" (v. 23). We have already seen how Paul identifies Christ with "firstfruits," thereby connecting his resurrection to the resurrection of all believers. Here, Paul assigns the same term to the Spirit, indicating that the Spirit, already possessed by believers, firmly connects them to the glory that will be theirs when Christ returns.

Contemporary Relevance: Paul's words in Romans 8:14-27 are incredibly rich, but we will limit our reflection to two key insights.

1) *Creation participates in our salvation.* Verse 19 insists that as we wait for the glory that is to come, all creation waits with us. At our death we hope for union with God in heaven. But heaven is not the end of our story. When Christ returns at the end of time, we believe that our present bodies will be transformed into glorified bodies. We also believe that all that God has made will be transformed by the Spirit. Somehow, animals, plants, mountains, and stars will all participate in the victory of

Christ. Nothing will be left behind. God will be "all in all" (1 Cor 15:28).

All too often we limit the work of the Spirit to our personal lives. Within this narrow perspective, the world in which we live can appear expendable, temporary, an extraneous dwelling we leave behind when we die. But Paul's gospel insists that the created world has an eternal future. Our honest efforts to curb the effects of global warming, end the pollution of our air and water, and rethink our treatment of animals as an expendable commodity are concrete signs of the respect that the created world deserves. The gospel calls us to recognize our planet as our common home. All that God has made will join us in a new creation.

 In 2015 Pope Francis issued his second encyclical letter, entitled **Laudato Si'** (Italian for "Praise Be to You"). It bears the subtitle "On Care for Our Common Home." *Laudato Si'* is a lengthy and comprehensive summary of the church's stance on environmental issues. Recognizing that our world is in the midst of an ecological crisis, Pope Francis calls Catholics to a profound interior conversion—to renew our relationships with God, one another, and the created world. Because of our belief in God as Creator, we understand that the created world has been entrusted to us as a gift. Because of the Christian gospel, we recognize that creation has an eternal future. Therefore, we have the responsibility to care for and protect all God has made.

2) *The Spirit groans with us.* As we wait in an "in between" time, Paul knows that suffering continues (v. 18). Caught between the "already" and the "not yet," many things are unclear and difficult. We do not fully understand God's plan or how it will come about. We are often dismayed by the injustices that surround us and devastated by the losses that harm us and those we love. We may even begin to question whether God's promises to us can be trusted. In such circumstances we may be unable to pray or even formulate a way to complain. We may find ourselves paralyzed by pain and confusion.

In response to such helplessness, God's Spirit is not passive. In a unique insight, Paul says that the Spirit groans with us (v. 26). This startling image is comforting but also deeply perceptive. The Spirit does not always resolve our doubts or remove our pain. The Spirit does not reveal to us the particulars of God's plan by explaining why bad things happen or why the innocent suffer. What the Spirit does is more surprising and intimate. It identifies with our shattered spirits and begins to moan with us, echoing our aimless cries and carrying them to the heart of God. And because the Spirit is God's Spirit, our emptiness and questioning are transfigured. Our inarticulate anguish becomes acceptable to God. Our wordless confusion becomes something holy. The broken pieces of our lives are taken up in the Spirit's own voice, transforming our groaning into an appeal, our pain into a prayer.

*　*　*　*　*　*

The six lessons of this study have traced the trajectory of God's Spirit in the Bible. We have seen how the Spirit creates and re-creates, inspires individuals, dwells within God's people, guides Jesus' ministry, empowers the church, and is both a present possession and a promise of what is to come. Promise is an appropriate place to conclude our study. The Spirit who promises us a glorious future is also the One who stands with us in our pain. This is God's gift at its most personal. The Spirit is the very breath of God within us, grounding our faith and hope, providing light and fire, coming to expression in words and groanings, but always binding us closer to the God who is saving us in Christ Jesus.

EXPLORING LESSON SIX

1. According to Paul's understanding of the gospel, why is Jesus' resurrection good news for us? In what way does Paul's perspective enlarge the gospel beyond our personal salvation (see commentary on 1 Cor 15:12-18)?

_____

_____

_____

_____

_____

2. Christian faith demands a balance between the salvation already accomplished in Christ and the final salvation that is not yet present. What happens when the "already" of Christ's victory is overemphasized? What happens when the "not yet" is made too much a focus?

_____

_____

_____

_____

_____

3. First Corinthians 2:9-13 assures us that the Spirit allows us to know God not through human wisdom but through words taught by the Spirit. Can you identify a time when you simply knew through a sense or prompting that something was good or right? Did you recognize that sense as a gift of God's Spirit?

_____

_____

_____

_____

4. Second Corinthians 3:1-6 reminds us that it is through the Spirit that we are able to serve others. Were you ever aware that your ability to help someone in need was successful more because of God's grace than your own efforts? Please relate the circumstances of the event.

_____

_____

_____

_____

_____

5. How would you explain Paul's understanding of "flesh" and "spirit" (see commentary on Rom 8:5-13)? Why does Paul believe that it is possible for us to be "in the flesh" and "in the spirit" at the same time?

_____

_____

_____

_____

_____

6. Five characteristics were enumerated in this lesson to describe Paul's understanding of the Body of Christ. Did any of these surprise you? Which, in your opinion, is the most important?

_____

_____

_____

_____

7. Paul insists that not all gifts of the Spirit are equal among the members of the Body of Christ. There is, however, a kind of equality in the body. How would you explain this equality in your own words or in your own experience? How important do you feel this equality is for us to function as a church?

_____

_____

_____

_____

8. Calling the Spirit a "first installment" connects the Spirit to the future (2 Cor 1:21-22; 5:5; see section "Not Yet: The Spirit as Promise"). What does the Spirit, as first installment, promise us? How is the Spirit's promise connected to all creation? Does Paul's teaching here offer you any new perspectives or insights?

_____

_____

_____

_____

9. Romans 8:26 claims that God's Spirit is groaning with us and with all creation. What are we groaning about? Do you find the image of groaning an effective one to describe a relationship with God's Spirit? Why or why not?

_____

_____

_____

_____

_____

_____

10. Reflecting back on your study of the Holy Spirit in the Bible, what images or ideas resonated with you the most? How might what you have learned about the Spirit enhance your relationship with God and others going forward?

_____

_____

_____

_____

_____

_____

CLOSING PRAYER

Prayer

[T]he fruit of the Spirit is love, joy, peace, patience, kindness, generosity, faithfulness, gentleness, self-control. (Gal 5:22-23)

Come, Holy Spirit, pour into our hearts your sacred gifts. Give us the wisdom to be aware of them and the strength to use them for the sake of the gospel. May we be loving, joyful, and peaceful; patient, kind, and generous; faithful, gentle, and governed by self-control. And in this way, with your help, may we imitate our Lord Jesus Christ, our Savior and brother. Today we pray for one another, especially . . .

PRAYING WITH YOUR GROUP

Because we know that the Bible allows us to hear God's voice, prayer provides the context for our study and sharing. By speaking and listening to God and each other, the discussion often grows to more deeply bond us to one another and to God.

At *the beginning and end of each lesson* simple prayers are provided for individual use, and also may be used within the group setting. Most of the closing prayers provided with each lesson relate directly to a theme from that lesson and encourage you to pray together for people and events in your local community.

Of course, there are many ways to center ourselves in God's presence as we gather together in groups around the word of God. We provide some additional suggestions here knowing you and your group will make prayer a priority as part of your gathering. These are simply alternative ways to pray if your group would like to try something different from those prayers provided in the previous pages.

Conversational Prayer

This form of prayer allows for the group members to pray in their own words in a way that is not intimidating. The group leader begins with Step One, inviting all to focus on the presence of Christ among them. After a few moments of quiet, the group leader invites anyone in the group to voice a prayer or two of thanksgiving; once that is complete, then anyone who has personal intentions may pray in their own words for their needs; finally, the group prays for the needs of others.

A suggested process:
In your own words, speak simple and short prayers to allow time for others to add their voices.

Focus on one "step" at a time, not worrying about praying for everything in your mental list at once.

Step One	Visualize Christ. Welcome him.
	Imagine him present with you in your group.
	Allow time for some silence.
Step Two	Gratitude opens our hearts.
	Use simple words such as, "Thank you, Lord, for . . ."
Step Three	Pray for your own needs knowing that others will pray with you.
	Be specific and honest.
	Use "I" and "me" language.

Step Four	Pray for others by name, with love. You may voice your agreement ("Yes, Lord"). End with gratitude for sharing concerns.

Praying Like Ignatius

St. Ignatius Loyola, whose life and ministry are the foundation of the Jesuit community, invites us to enter into Scripture texts in order to experience the scenes, especially scenes of the Gospels or other narrative parts of Scripture. Simply put, this is a method of creatively imagining the scene, viewing it from the inside, and asking God to meet you there. Most often, this is a personal form of prayer, but in a group setting, some of its elements can be helpful if you allow time for this process.

A suggested process:

- Select a scene from the chapters in the particular lesson.

- Read that scene out loud in the group, followed by some quiet time.

- Ask group members to place themselves in the scene (as a character, or as an onlooker) so that they can imagine the emotions, responses, and thinking that may have taken place. Notice the details and the tone, and imagine the interaction with the Lord that is taking place.

- Share with the group any insights that came to you in this quiet imagining.

- Allow each person in the group to thank God for some insight and to pray about some request that may have surfaced.

Sacred Reading (or Lectio Divina)

This method of prayer invites us to "listen with the ear of the heart" as St. Benedict's rule would say. We listen to the words and the phrasing, asking God to speak to our innermost being. Again, this method of prayer is most often used in an individual setting but may also be used in an adapted way within a group.

A suggested process:

- Select a scene from the chapters in the particular lesson.

- Read the scene out loud in the group, perhaps two times.

- Ask group members to ponder a word or phrase that stands out to them.

- The group members could then simply speak the word or phrase as a kind of litany of what was meaningful for your group.

- Allow time for more silence to ponder the words that were heard, asking God to reveal to you what message you are meant to hear, how God is speaking to you.

- Follow up with spoken intentions at the close of this group time.

REFLECTING ON SCRIPTURE

Reading Scripture is an opportunity not simply to learn new information but to listen to God who loves you. Pray that the same Holy Spirit who guided the formation of Scripture will inspire you to correctly understand what you read, and empower you to make what you read a part of your life.

The inspired word of God contains layers of meaning. As you make your way through passages of Scripture, whether studying a book of the Bible or focusing on a biblical theme, you may find it helpful to ask yourself these four questions:

What does the Scripture passage say?
Read the passage slowly and reflectively. Become familiar with it. If the passage you are reading is a narrative, carefully observe the characters and the plot. Use your imagination to picture the scene or enter into it.

What does the Scripture passage mean?
Read the footnotes in your Bible and the commentary provided to help you understand what the sacred writers intended and what God wants to communicate by means of their words.

What does the Scripture passage mean to me?
Meditate on the passage. God's word is living and powerful. What is God saying to you? How does the Scripture passage apply to your life today?

What am I going to do about it?
Try to discover how God may be challenging you in this passage. An encounter with God contains a challenge to know God's will and follow it more closely in daily life. Ask the Holy Spirit to inspire not only your mind but your life with this living word.